Growing Leaders:

Empowering Leadership and Management Skills in Your Teenage Child

By: Mustafa Nejem

Foreword

Dear Readers,

As parents, educators, and mentors, we constantly seek ways to equip our youth with the skills and mindset necessary to thrive in an ever-evolving world. In "Growing Leaders: Empowering Leadership and Management Skills in Your Teenage Child,"

As we move further into the technological age, leadership skills have become increasingly important for our teenage children to develop. In this book, the author provides a comprehensive guide for parents and teenagers seeking to cultivate strong leadership abilities through meaningful lessons and examples.

Across 20 insightful chapters, readers are taken on an enriching journey that explores the timeless principles of leadership and modern approaches relevant to today's world. Starting with defining leadership and evaluating one's innate characteristics, it compares different leadership styles, emphasizes the importance of communication and decision-making, and examines valuable skills like conflict resolution, teamwork, and time management.

Interspersed case studies of successful young leaders and thought-provoking exercises help bring the concepts to life. Teenagers will appreciate relatable anecdotes while gaining self-awareness. Parents will find discussion points to engage their children in leadership development. Later chapters delve into important soft skills, ethical considerations, public speaking tips, and the role of parents, mentors, and community in nurturing leadership qualities from a young age.

In an increasingly volatile, uncertain, complex, and ambiguous environment, this comprehensive guidebook equips teens with the confidence and know-how to take up leadership roles. It also aids parents in raising dynamic, empathetic, and service-oriented leaders of tomorrow. With technology rapidly shaping the future, nurturing qualities like emotional intelligence, adaptability, inclusive thinking, and digital communication becomes essential for future-ready leaders.

This book serves as a valuable resource for anyone seeking to embark on a transformational journey of empowering their innate leadership potential and making a positive difference. I highly recommend it to parents, educators, and progressive teenagers committed to developing into well-rounded, principled leaders.

Table of Content

Introduction

Welcome to "Growing Leaders," a comprehensive guide to help nurture leadership skills in teenagers. As you begin this journey of self-discovery, I encourage you to go through each chapter with an open and reflective mindset. Question beliefs, explore new perspectives, and assimilate learning into real-world action.

Leadership is a continually evolving concept with no set definition. However, at its core lies the ability to positively influence, inspire, and empower people to achieve common goals. Effective leaders drive meaningful change through strong character, clear vision, communication mastery, diplomacy, and more. They emerge from situations better than before by learning from failures and celebrating victories together with the team.

This book touches upon timeless principles of exemplary leadership while also addressing contemporary skills demanded by the VUCA (Volatility, Uncertainty, Complexity, And Ambiguity) world we live in. It examines not just what leadership entails but also how to consistently develop and strengthen these competencies from a young age. Each chapter is designed to help you gain self-awareness, evaluate different approaches and leadership styles, and give actionable tips to enhance your strengths.

While focusing on personal growth, the book also touches upon pivotal supporting roles that parents, mentors, and the community play in nurturing future leaders. It debunks stereotypes that certain qualities are innate rather than cultivated. With the right mindset and efforts over time, anyone can build exceptional leadership potential.

I invite you to make the most of this opportunity by reflecting deeply on guided discussions and applying learnings proactively. Wishing you the very best on this meaningful journey of transformation that will surely empower you to rise as an ethical, inclusive, and service-oriented leader.

Chapter **1**

What is Leadership?

The concept of leadership has evolved tremendously over the years from a position of unilateral authority to a more collaborative and service-oriented approach. In ancient times, leadership emerged from military dominance where might was right. Leaders commanded obedience through force and centralization of power. However, as civilizations progressed, leadership theories started incorporating aspects of cooperation, empathy, and moral responsibility.

In the industrial age during the early 20th century, leadership was viewed through the lens of "the great man theory," where exceptional qualities of an individual set them apart as a natural-born leader. Traits like intelligence, self-confidence, and personality were believed to define a leader. This trait-based approach was later criticized for ignoring situational factors and not considering how behaviors impact followers. As organizations grew complex post World War 2, leadership models shifted to focus on behaviors through styles like authoritarian, democratic, and laissez-faire.

Contemporary views see leadership as an inclusive process where the leader acts as a role model to empower followers toward collective goals. Situational and transformational approaches highlight adapting one's style based on team dynamics and needs. With rapid technology changes, the VUCA world demands leaders to cultivate agility and resilience and embrace diversity & ambiguity. Today's leaders facilitate knowledge sharing, encourage innovative thinking, and drive meaningful change through collaboration rather than commandeering.

Looking ahead, to succeed in exponential times, future leaders will need to nurture a learning mindset, strengthen emotional intelligence, and think frugally with limited resources. As artificial intelligence supplants routine jobs, the uniquely human skills of empathy, judgment, and creativity will become increasingly important. Success will rely on building a cohesive purpose, gaining trust through transparency, and empowering others to lead. In such a dynamic environment, leadership is a lifelong journey of continuous self-improvement rather than a destination to reach.

The characteristics expected from leaders have significantly evolved across different decades to reflect the changing societal and business landscape. In the 1900s, leaders were expected to be strong-willed, assertive, and directive in their approach. Masculine traits like dominance, physical courage, and competitiveness were highly valued.

In the 1950s-60s, as organizations grew larger post-World War 2, the focus shifted to projecting a charismatic personality with clear communication. Leaders were seen as inspirational visionaries who could strategize and get the best out of large workforces. Traits like public speaking abilities and ambition came to the fore.

During the 1970s-80s, the increasing pace of globalization made collaboration and social skills crucial. Leaders were expected to be team players, consensus-builders, and empowering coaches who treated people with respect. Interpersonal skills like active listening, emotional intelligence, and diplomacy became important alongside strategic thinking.

Post the Millennium, technology disruptions, networked economies, and transnational issues demand current leaders to be agile networkers. They exhibit flexibility and resilience in unstable environments. Strengths like digital literacy, multicultural awareness, and community building are essential for building online and offline communities.

Looking ahead, future leaders are envisioned to be inclusive problem-solvers, systems-thinkers, and lifelong learners, given exponential changes. While self-awareness, integrity, and vision will remain foundational, futuristic traits like curiosity, adaptability, frugal innovation, and comfort with ambiguity may define successful leaders tomorrow in the VUCA world.

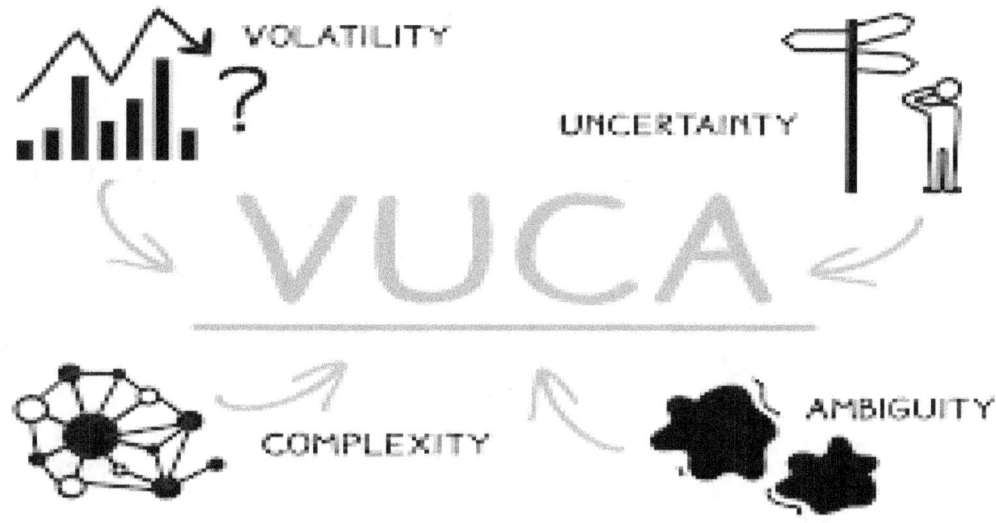

Self-Assessment Activity

The purpose of this short activity is to gain more self-awareness about leadership strengths and aspects to improve. Answer questions honestly based on how you see yourself currently.

Part 1

Rate yourself on a scale of 1-10 (where 1=low and 10=high) for each characteristic:

- Communication skills
- Problem-solving ability
- Teamwork skills
- Self-confidence
- Work ethic
- Reliability
- Initiative
- Public speaking
- Vision/strategic thinking
- Kindness towards others

Part 2

List 3 things you are naturally good at. How can these strengths be assets for leadership?

Part 3

List 1-2 areas you can work to improve. What specific steps will you take over the next month to strengthen these?

Part 4

What motivates you? Is it achievements, relationships, or making an impact? How can understanding your drivers help maximize your strengths?

Part 5

Name 3 leaders you admire and why. What qualities inspire you that you can inculcate?

Part 6

Based on your self-reflection, which leadership roles do you think you are best suited for now - like team projects, community initiatives, etc.? How will taking on these help your journey?

This self-assessment is a starting point to gain clarity. Revisit it periodically to track your progress, along with feedback from others. Identifying your leadership potential is the first step to cultivating it.

Case Studies of Young Leaders

Lucas Duplan

Lucas Duplan is a young French entrepreneur who co-founded the AI safety startup Anthropic at the age of 21. Ever since his childhood, Lucas has been fascinated by technology and believes in its potential to help humanity. He studied Machine Learning and Computer Science at university, graduating at the age of 20. During his final year project, Lucas realized that there was a lack of research being done in the important field of AI safety as the technology progressed. He felt compelled to dedicate his skills and efforts to solving this challenge. In 2018, right after graduating, Lucas co-founded Anthropic with Dario Amodei. Through his technical expertise and visionary leadership, he helped the fledgling startup secure $5 million in seed funding. Under Lucas' guidance, key processes and infrastructure were established during the crucial early months. Over the next few years, Anthropic grew exponentially under his leadership. The team expanded to 50 members, conducting cutting-edge research on beneficial AI techniques. Lucas successfully raised $30 million in Series A funding to vastly scale up Anthropic's impactful work. He has also represented the startup at various global tech forums to raise awareness about existential AI risk.

Rebecca Zash

Rebecca Zash is an American entrepreneur who founded the AI hiring platform Zety at just 16 years of age. Born in 2001, Rebecca had always been passionate about technology and saw how coding could help streamline inefficient processes. She taught herself to code and build websites from a young age. In 2017, after realizing the flaws in traditional hiring, Rebecca created the initial prototype for Zety. Through self-funded development and refinements based on user feedback, she improved the AI-powered hiring platform. Determined to solve the problem at scale, Rebecca made the bold decision to drop out of high school in her senior year and focus full-time on growing Zety. Within the first year, the startup saw tremendous traction, with over 1000 customers and more than 1 million job listings on the platform. This success helped Rebecca raise $2 million in seed funding. Over the next few years, under her strong leadership, Zety processed millions of resumes for over 5000 companies worldwide. Rebecca's technical skills and entrepreneurial success led to her being named to the prestigious Forbes 30 Under 30 list in 2022. She exemplifies the positive impact young leaders can make through passion and determination.

Chapter **2**

Valley of Leadership

There are various approaches a leader can take when guiding their team towards goals and visions. Understanding the different leadership styles is an important early step for gaining awareness of how one's innate inclinations may manifest, as well as determining the optimal approach depending on contextual demands. Broadly, three primary styles emerge - autocratic, democratic, and laissez-faire. The autocratic leader maintains tight control through top-down directives and central decision-making without input from followers. While suitable in times that require rapid response to critical issues, long-term outcomes tend to see less buy-in and satisfaction due to the lack of empowerment this approach fosters.

On the opposite end of the spectrum is the laissez-faire style, wherein leaders offer minimal guidance, allowing teams high autonomy in decision rights and work processes. This cultivates independence and responsibility, but not having sufficient coordination can lead to a lack of focus or missed deadlines. Finding a balanced middle path, the democratic leader engages their team collaboratively to gather ideas, provide feedback, and gain consensus on the best path ahead. Though more time-intensive in fast-paced scenarios, the participative nature of this style helps develop loyal and innovative teams through nurturing shared ownership and empowerment. Truly skilled leaders understand knowing when and how to adjust depending on the demands at hand, flexing between fully autonomous directives to fully engaged collaboration to best accomplish goals through motivating people.

There are various approaches leaders can take to guide, motivate, and direct their teams toward achieving strategic objectives and realizing an organizational vision. Understanding different leadership styles provides crucial self-awareness and contextual insight for developing one's abilities. At a fundamental level, three primary styles emerge - autocratic, democratic, and laissez-faire.

The autocratic style is characterized by a top-down, directive approach where decision-making power is centralized within the leader. Communication flows solely from the leader down to followers, without active solicitation of ideas or feedback from team members. While effective in crisis situations demanding swift action, this authoritarian approach often breeds disengagement long-term. Without empowerment or investment in the process, commitment and creativity tend to wane over time.

In contrast, the laissez-faire style adopts a hands-off philosophy where leaders provide minimal direction while allowing high autonomy to team members over decision rights and work processes. This cultivates independence, but without sufficient guidance or coordination from the leader, efforts risk becoming scattered, or deadlines missed as accountability is diffuse.

Striking a balanced middle ground is the democratic leadership style. Democratic leaders engage their teams collaboratively and are consensus-driven. Input is actively gathered from team members to inform decisions through an interactive two-way communication style. While participation leads to shared ownership and empowerment, fostering long-term innovation and productivity, the process can be time-intensive in volatile environments requiring prompt responses.

Truly agile leaders understand no singular approach applies to every situation and purposefully flex between styles based on assessed parameters like the nature of the task, competencies within the team, the urgency of timelines, and organizational dynamics at play. Effectiveness lies in self-awareness of one's natural inclinations, in addition to the adaptive capacity to alternate modalities when situational demands necessitate an alternate approach for optimal outcomes.

There are several different leadership styles that leaders can adopt, each with their own pros and cons. The autocratic style centralizes all power and decision-making with the leader. While this allows for quick decisions in times of crisis, it often leads to low employee morale and a lack of innovation as their input is not valued. A democratic style encourages participation and consensus building, boosting employee motivation and commitment. However, decisions can be slow, and debates dragging. The laissez-faire style gives employees freedom and flexibility, but with little guidance, they may feel lost without clear direction.

The transactional style uses positive and negative reinforcement tied to clear expectations and objectives, motivating employees to achieve goals. However, it is short-term focused without the development of intrinsic motivation or individual growth. The transformational style inspires employees through influence rather than authority, developing future leaders while building long-term organizational commitments. While this promotes innovation and problem-solving, it requires strong charismatic leadership skills and individualized attention that can be challenging to provide across large organizations.

In summary, the appropriate leadership style depends on factors like the organization's goals, stage of development, and company culture. Effective leaders understand the pros and cons of different approaches and adapt their style based on specific situational needs, integrating aspects of various styles for optimal outcomes. No single approach is perfect for all situations, and flexibility is important.

There are several theoretical models that attempt to explain different aspects of the complex phenomenon of leadership. Among the earliest and most influential is the trait model, which identifies distinct personality traits and characteristics commonly seen in successful leaders. However, it is now recognized that traits alone do not guarantee leadership, as situational factors also play a role. In response, contingency models emerged, stressing that effective leadership depends on matching leadership styles to contextual variables. For example, Fiedler's contingency theory identifies relationship-oriented and task-oriented styles and their appropriateness based on factors like control over the situation and leader-member relations.

The path-goal theory builds on this, addressing how leaders can help followers achieve goals by selecting behaviors that cater to their needs and environmental demands. Transformational leadership theory then shifted the focus to the leader's ability to inspire and motivate followers through influence rather than authority. More recently, adaptive leadership has gained prominence, recognizing that many challenges lack clear solutions, requiring leaders to help others adapt. Similarly, complexity theory views leadership as an emergent, dynamic process with unpredictable outcomes rather than a set of skills. Servant leadership puts serving followers' needs as the priority over asserting control and power.

Each model offers indispensable insights but is limited in scope as well. An integrated approach combining relevant aspects seems most effective for comprehending leadership holistically across diverse contexts. Further research continues refining models and testing them in new situations to advance the evolving understanding of this immensely important phenomenon impacting all organizations.

Did You Know?

"5% of Fortune 500 companies look for leadership qualities over specific job skills or experiences when hiring new graduates."

Chapter **3**

Leadership & Communication

"A Perfect Quest"

Verbal and non-verbal communication skills are both important for effective leadership. Strong verbal skills involve active listening, public speaking ability, and articulating ideas clearly and concisely. Leaders must be careful about the words they use, as language can empower or discourage followers. They should ask open-ended questions to encourage input and provide constructive feedback to facilitate growth. Non-verbal communication, which accounts for over 50% of social messages exchanged, also significantly impacts leadership presence. Facial expressions, body language, eye contact, and physical distance all convey attitudes and influence perceptions.

Posture, gestures, and tone of voice can communicate confidence, build rapport, and engage audiences. Smiling, maintaining an open stance, and mirroring others' non-verbal behaviors help establish understanding and rapport. Conversely, crossed arms, poor eye contact, and fidgeting may undermine credibility. Cultural differences also affect non-verbal norms, so cultural competence is important. Touch requires careful consideration depending on the context, as excessive or lacking touch could negatively impact relationships. Leaders must be mindful that non-verbal channels often contradict or reinforce verbal messages. Together, strong verbal delivery and aligned non-verbal presence allow leaders to effectively inspire people with their vision, resolve misunderstandings, and rally support for initiatives through influential communication. Developing both sets of skills is vital for leadership success in any environment.

Tips to Develop Active Listening Skills in Teenagers

It is important to teach teenagers active listening skills that they can carry into adulthood. Some effective ways to do this include modeling active listening behaviors as a parent. Make eye contact with them, turn off distractions, and focus entirely on what they are saying without interrupting. Reflect back on what they said to ensure you understand their perspective. Ask thoughtful questions to gain more clarity or have them expand on certain points. Validate their feelings to show empathy.

Encourage teens to practice these same active listening skills with friends. Suggest they restate what the other person said to check their understanding. Suggestions like "it sounds like you felt frustrated when..." can help teens listen for emotions behind the words. Role-playing scenarios where one is the speaker and the other the active listener reinforces the techniques in a low-pressure way. Point out when they catch themselves making assumptions instead of asking questions. Compliment their efforts each time you notice them engaged in true listening.

Teach teens to be aware of body language cues, too, since much is communicated nonverbally. Maintaining eye contact, facing the speaker, and nodding to show interest are all part of active participation. By developing strong listening comprehension at a younger age, teens will be prepared to have more meaningful discussions and resolve conflicts constructively as they get older. Active listening is an invaluable lifelong communication skill.

Exercises for leadership skills development in teenagers

Role-playing allows teens to practice leadership skills in a low-pressure environment.

Some effective scenarios include:

Meeting facilitation

One teen leads a mock student club meeting, creating an agenda and encouraging participation. Others take roles like note-takers, timers, etc. The leader practices keeping things on track, involving, and wrapping up.

Collaborative problem-solving

In groups, teens are given dilemmas to solve together, like organizing a charity fundraiser or resolving a disagreement between friends. Rotate leadership to give everyone a turn directing discussion and consensus-building.

Delegating tasks

For an imaginary event, have teens work in committees led by a rotating project manager overseeing timelines and deliverables. This teaches assigning roles appropriately and holding peers accountable.

Managing disagreement

Role-play debates where the leader must hear different perspectives fairly and bring the group to a decision. This develops conflict resolution skills.

Effective feedback

Scenarios like performance reviews teach leaders to appropriately deliver positive and corrective feedback respectfully and constructively.

Public speaking

Simulate situations like presentations, where a teen must communicate goals clearly, engage an audience, and field questions confidently.

Role-playing makes leadership intangible skills more tangible and accessible for youth to practice. Guidance and structured scenarios can boost the self-awareness and competence of emerging leaders.

Case Studies

Jeff Bezos-Amazon

Jeff Bezos has built Amazon into one of the world's most valuable and innovative companies through his visionary leadership. From the start, he established a culture of customer obsession, where decisions are made to benefit customers above all else. Bezos is also famously data-driven, wanting to base choices on rigorous analysis rather than gut feeling.

He fosters an inventive, risk-taking culture where employees are encouraged to fail fast and learn from mistakes. Bezos personally reviews every significant product or initiative with questions probing for weaknesses to preempt issues. He empowers leaders with autonomy as long as they share his long-term experimentation mindset.

Bezos leads by example with his curiosity, work ethic, and emotional intelligence. He regularly solicits critical feedback and challenges even from junior employees, knowing conversations improve with diverse views. Bezos believes in appropriately deferring to experts while informing decisions with his experienced, holistic perspective.

His "disagree and commit" model for respectful debate inspires others to rigorously interrogate options without bruised egos. Teams then unitedly drive choices forward. Bezos believes that long-term success requires optimizing for customers today while envisioning future consumer needs.

Now, the focus shifts to Amazon's next act, from delivering packages to machine learning/robotics. Bezos' investor mindset of maximizing shareholder value positions Amazon well for future growth through prudent exploration and bold experimentation. His vision and talent for systematically reinventing customer experiences make him one of history's most impactful CEOs.

At Amazon, Jeff Bezos fosters a culture of "disagree and commit," where intense debates of ideas are encouraged to surface the best solutions. By welcoming challenges from employees and embracing diverse perspectives, better decisions are made that consider all angles and risks. Once the discussion concludes, everyone then fully commits to supporting the agreed path forward. This has allowed Amazon to sustain high levels of innovation while ensuring strategic alignment. During the COVID-19 pandemic, New Zealand Prime Minister Jacinda Ardern similarly took a collaborative stance. She involved medical experts extensively from the outset to shape evidence-based policies.

Additionally, keeping open channels of communication through public briefings and stakeholder roundtables ensured policies accounted for all realities and maintained public confidence. This collaborative approach with diverse inputs crafted restrictions that maximized compliance, which was critical for flattening the curve. Both case studies exemplify how valuing collaborative decision-making through respectful debate and two-way communication can help drive improved outcomes, especially in complex, high-stakes environments.

Steve Jobs-Apple

Steve Jobs was a visionary leader who transformed multiple industries through his innovative products and business approach at Apple. He had a clear vision for Apple's philosophy of elegantly integrating hardware, software, and digital content. Jobs paid close attention to every detail of products and user experience. He surrounded himself with A-players, empowering his top executives to lead their areas with autonomy as long as it aligned with his vision.

Jobs fostered a culture of pushing boundaries and challenging the status quo. He encouraged employees to openly debate ideas until the best solution emerged. Despite his demanding nature, people were motivated by Jobs' passion and willingness to take risks for excellence. When projects went off course, he stepped in decisively to reset direction. Under Jobs, Apple prioritized secrecy to protect new ideas, keeping even executives in silos to curb leaks.

While Jobs could be brutally honest in criticism, he also inspired fierce loyalty in teams through his leadership. He united Apple's diverse departments to collaboratively deliver his idealized whole product experiences ahead of competitors. Jobs deeply understood users and shaped products to meet their needs before they knew it themselves. His showmanship in unveiling innovations made Apple a cultural phenomenon.

Steve Jobs was renowned for surrounding himself with highly capable direct reports and empowering them to lead their areas with vision and autonomy. However, he provided strong oversight and direction to integrate efforts into Apple's unified brand. During the Gulf oil spill, BP CEO Tony Hayward collaborated vigorously with response agencies, scientists, and local stakeholders to mobilize the largest cleanup in history through shared leadership. At Southwest Airlines, Herb Kelleher fostered an inclusive, team-oriented culture where employees at all levels feel a sense of shared ownership over the company's success. This has kept morale and performance high for decades.

After over a decade away, Jobs returned and successfully led Apple's resurgence through accountability, focus on only a few products at a time, and unwavering commitment to excellence over profit or deadlines. His vision, demanding drive for perfection, and ability to galvanize creativity made Steve Jobs one of history's most transformational and influential business leaders.

Chapter **4**

A Teenager's Psyche

During the turbulent period of adolescence, a teenager experiences immense changes both physically and emotionally as they transition into adulthood. Within their developing psyche, core elements that influence leadership potential begin to emerge. On the cognitive level, abstract and complex thought processes allow teens to consider multiple perspectives as well as hypothetical scenarios. Their rapidly maturing prefrontal cortex cultivates creativity, strategic thinking, and sound decision-making even when emotions run high. Socially, teenagers strive for independence while craving approval from their peers. For many, this drives a desire to rally others around a cause or idea. Their innate rebellious spirit and willingness to challenge the status quo provide fuel for positive change. When channeled constructively, a teen's emotional intensity and passion can inspire others. Their evolving identity and self-awareness during this pivotal stage cultivate strong communication skills and empathy. Even in the face of uncertainty, adapting to constant change promotes resilience and an ability to influence direction. Therefore, while teenage years may bring angst and impulsiveness, a discerning look reveals the budding leadership qualities within. Traits like vision, courage, charisma, and work ethic can emerge if guided toward serving the collective interests of the community.

The teenage years mark a transformation from childhood to adulthood as one's psyche develops in complexity. On the cognitive level, abstract thinking enables teens to consider multiple perspectives simultaneously. Their prefrontal cortex, the center of reasoning and complex thought, undergoes significant maturation. While this gives rise to creativity, strategic thinking, and sound decision-making even in emotionally charged situations, it also means adolescent brains are not fully formed. Teens exhibit heightened risk-taking behaviors and impulsivity due to an imbalance between developing prefrontal control systems and reward systems fully online.

Socially and emotionally, the quest for independence clashes with the desire for peer approval and acceptance. This activates the limbic reward system intensely, driving teenagers to rally others to their causes in hopes of belonging. Their rebellious spirit emerges from pushing boundaries as they differentiate from their parents. When channeled positively, a teen's passion and emotional intensity can be inspirational. Navigating this period of constant internal and external change cultivates resilience through learning to adapt.

As identity evolves, interpersonal skills like communication and empathy strengthen through deepening self-awareness and understanding others. Vision, courage, and enthusiasm emerge from exploring interests and discovering purpose. Charisma develops by embracing individuality while building connections. Work ethic increases by persevering through challenges. If guided constructively, these innate leadership characteristics can emerge from within the ever changing teenage psyche to positively impact the community when serving collective interests rather than solely the self. Overall, adolescence lays the groundwork for future leadership potential through cognitive, social, and emotional learning experiences.

Do's and Don'ts of Parent's guidance to Mold, the leaders in Their Children

Do's

> Encourage independent thinking and responsible risk-taking within safe limits to build confidence. Discuss alternatives and consequences.

> Express belief in their abilities and potential while providing thoughtful feedback on strengths and areas for growth. Praise effort over outcomes.

> Involve them in family/community activities and voluntary work to discover passions and develop empathy. Lead by example with positivity and integrity.

> Allow input in age-appropriate decision-making to practice leadership skills like delegation, problem-solving, and compromise.

> Foster open communication through respectful listening without judgment. Create a safe space to freely discuss ideas, emotions, and challenges.

Don'ts

> Micromanage or be overprotective. Helicopter parenting stunts the development of independence required for leadership roles.

> Be overly critical, especially concerning interests, appearance, or normal teenage behaviors within reason. This breeds low self-esteem.

> Dismiss ideas, wants, or friends just because you disagree. Consider different perspectives and facilitate respectful discussions.

- ➢ Neglect responsibilities as a parent by being a "friend." Clear boundaries and logical consequences are still needed.
- ➢ Compare them to others or have unrealistic expectations of perfectionism. Celebrate effort and progress over results to build resilience through setbacks.
- ➢ Be passive or hands-off. Teens need structure, mentorship, and guidance in life skills to become socially responsible leaders.

The key is providing scaffolding through engaged support and empowerment versus dictating direction or trying to live vicariously through them.

Case Studies of Psychological Evolution

Case Study 1:

John was shy and insecure in middle school. He struggled socially and lacked the confidence to pursue his interests in music and environmental activism. In high school, John joined the school band and debate club, where he found peer support and began coming out of his shell. His debate coach recognized John's intellectual abilities and passion for the environment. She mentored him in running for VP of the club, where he had to give speeches. This pushed John out of his comfort zone. Although nervous, he focused on his message and connected with classmates through shared values. John became more assured in his ideas and abilities. As VP, he organized fundraisers and community cleanups that gained momentum. John's resilience in overcoming social anxiety and pursuit of his leadership potential resulted in him gaining popularity for positively impacting the school and getting elected student body president senior year.

Case Study 2:

Sara struggled with her parents' divorce in 8th grade, which caused trust issues. She acted out by breaking rules and distancing herself from school. A guidance counselor noticed Sara's creative skills and introduced her to the art club. There, Sara found an outlet and made supportive friends. In high school, Sara joined the student government to help cope with family issues. She had to learn teamwork and collaboration. Over time, Sara developed empathy for others going through hardships, like handling financial responsibilities at home, which shaped her determination. As president, Sara revitalized events through crowdsourcing new ideas. Her perseverance through personal adversity evolved Sara into a role model for her caring advocacy and transformative leadership abilities that left a lasting impact.

The Takeaways

- ✓ Teenagers thrive when their passions and talents are identified and encouraged through extracurricular activities. This boosts confidence and social skills.
- ✓ Overcoming shyness, self-doubt, or personal hardships helps build resilience, which is an important leadership trait. Mentorship can facilitate facing challenges.

- ✓ Taking on roles of responsibility such as officer positions within clubs pushes psychological growth by training public speaking, organization, and teamwork abilities.

- ✓ Staying engaged in school and community helps with coping mechanisms during turbulent adolescent periods. It can transform psychological setbacks into sources of strength.

- ✓ Perseverance, work ethic, and determination to positively impact others despite obstacles mark the evolution towards exemplary leadership qualities

- ✓ Leading by example through caring advocacy and crowdsourcing new ideas breeds popularity and leaves impacts that shape futures.

- ✓ Empathy develops from facing adversities, which cultivates socially responsible leadership styles.

- ✓ Multiple avenues need exploring to discover talents and foster interests crucial for adolescents' psychological well-being and emerging potential.

- ✓ Positive mentoring plays a key role by recognizing abilities, offering support, and challenging teenagers to step outside their comfort zones in low-risk environments.

Did You Know?

"Teenagers who practiced shared decision-making skills at home through things like family meetings are 3 times more likely to hold leadership roles at work as young adults."

Chapter **5**

A Balanced Decision-Making Realm-Supported by Leadership

Balanced decision-making refers to an approach where leaders consider all relevant perspectives and factors before arriving at a solution. Leaders need to make well-reasoned choices after weighing both pros and cons without letting biases or personal preferences skew the process. Some key tactics leaders employ for balanced decision-making include thorough research and information gathering from diverse sources, active listening to various stakeholder views without judgment, identifying clear criteria to evaluate options, separating facts from assumptions, and employing logic over emotions. Looking at short-term impacts alongside long-term implications is also crucial. Debate and discourse allow testing solutions from different angles to surface blind spots. Compromise and consensus-building tactics promote inclusion. Documenting the rationale for transparency builds trust.

Balanced decision-making is vital for effective leadership as it results in choices with widespread acceptance and support. One-sided or rushed decisions risk alienating important constituencies and missing valuable insight, potentially leading to poor outcomes or unintended consequences down the road. Seeking a variety of perspectives recognizes there are multiple ways to approach problems with no single right answer. This opens leaders to creative solutions and fortifies resolutions against future challenges. Treating all stakeholders with fairness and respect sets the example of even-handed leadership. Overall, taking the time for careful and methodical consideration of options through balanced decision-making strengthens integrity, legitimacy, and sound judgment—core attributes of trusted leaders.

Tactics:

- ✓ Establish a diverse decision-making team to bring different knowledge and perspectives. This prevents groupthink.
- ✓ Use data and facts to understand all dimensions of the problem/opportunity rather than relying on assumptions. Gather both quantitative and qualitative insights.
- ✓ Apply decision-making frameworks like plus/delta analysis, decision trees, or weighted scoring models to structure the evaluation process.

- ✓ Consider alternative futures and "what if" scenarios to analyze options under different potential conditions and outlier risks.
- ✓ Allow sufficient time for thorough discussion without feeling rushed before committing to a choice.

Importance for Leaders:

- ✓ It generates long-term sustainable solutions that address the real complexity of issues instead of superficial fixes.
- ✓ Employees and stakeholders have confidence in the leadership's impartial judgment and strategic thinking abilities.
- ✓ Balanced decisions tend to minimize unintended consequences since multiple angles have been factored in.
- ✓ The leader sets an example of inclusiveness, transparency, and integrity that permeates the organizational culture.
- ✓ It creates resilience and agility to changing circumstances since alternatives were fully vetted ahead of time.
- ✓ The decision's legitimacy enhances commitment to follow through on implementation even if difficulties arise.

Leaders rely on effective tactics to achieve balanced decision-making. Clearly defining the problem allows for objective consideration of alternatives rather than reactionary responses. Conducting research through stakeholder interviews and surveys ensures important viewpoints are recognized and represented in options. Brainstorming diverse ideas with an open mind prevents premature dismissal of valuable solutions that thinking outside the box could generate. Appointing a "devil's advocate" provides a critical lens to analyze each option's weaknesses, strengthening the final decision. Modeling transparency by thinking through the rationale behind the options selected invites productive feedback.

Numerically scoring alternatives according to predefined criteria takes subjectivity out of the analysis. Pilot testing top choices catch unintended issues before full-scale commitment. Periodic reevaluation maintains the decision's effectiveness over time by addressing new developments. These balanced tactics are vital for leaders as they foster comprehensive decisions supported by all stakeholders, thereby earning the organization-wide trust that leaders depend on to carry out their vision successfully. It also sets the example that fair processes form the basis of strong, resilient leadership.

Earns trust that all stakeholder needs have been reasonably addressed through a fair process. This trust is vital for leader legitimacy and results in buy-in for decision implementation. Considering diverse options prevents potential regret associated with neglecting an alternative solution that could have been highly successful. Critical analysis of each choice by challenging preconceived leanings results in decisions fortified against unforeseen obstacles. Numerical rating holds the analysis to objective criteria rather than subjective biases, giving leaders data-backed credibility and confidence in their choice. Testing choices early allows problems to be identified and addressed before scaling up, circumventing costly failures. Periodic reevaluation keeps performance on track by catching undesirable developments promptly. This ongoing improvement gives leaders flexibility to respond to a dynamic environment while maintaining stakeholder faith that their interests remain a priority. Overall, the balanced decision-making approach strengthens leaders' authority through demonstrated competence, integrity, and care for all impacted parties.

Being a strong decision-maker lays the foundation for becoming a successful leader. Teenagers who can make well-thought-out, balanced decisions demonstrate important leadership traits such as problem-solving skills, the ability to consider different perspectives, taking responsibility for outcomes, and setting an example through their judgment calls.

However, decision-making is just one aspect of leadership. Successful student leaders must also be able to inspire peers towards a shared vision, plan approaches to achieve goals, and coordinate team efforts. Decision-makers who can clearly communicate decisions and bring people together around solutions through their interpersonal skills are more effective at enacting change.

Additionally, the best student leaders make decisions with the cooperation and buy-in of their fellow members. Strong decision-makers who also foster an inclusive environment where others feel heard and valued are more likely to build trusting relationships that strengthen their leadership credibility.

Similarly, leaders who can acknowledge when a situation requires group consensus rather than top-down rulings maintain approachability. Decision fatigue is real for busy teenagers, so delegating appropriately paces themselves while developing followers' skills.

In summary, teenagers who couple polished independent decision-making with social competencies like collaboration, empathy, and motivation have greater leadership potential.

The most impactful student heads are proficient both at navigating issues and empowering their peers through a balanced cooperative-command dynamic.

Decision-making process to better depict leadership in young Adolescents

1. **Identifying the Issue:** Young teens are still sharpening their ability to clearly define problems. Leadership involves breaking down complex situations into manageable parts.

2. **Gathering Information:** Gathering diverse input challenges limited perspectives. Leaders source facts from various knowledgeable people.

3. **Brainstorming Options:** Imaginative idea generation comes easier to youth. Channeling creativity into workable solutions shows initiative.

4. **Evaluating Alternatives:** Weighing pros/cons introduces cost-benefit analysis. Lateral thinking tools like decision matrices appeal to logical teen minds.

5. **Making the Final Call:** Backing decisions with reasoned explanations builds self-assurance over time. Communicating transparently fosters accountability.

6. **Implementing the Plan:** Follow-through teaches that leadership involves rolling up sleeves to ensure visions materialize.

7. **Checking Progress:** The review allows course corrections when needed. The cycle of constant improvement readies youth for complex, real-world problems.

8. **Soliciting Feedback:** Openness to critique is a mark of strong yet humble leaders. Opinions of peers lend perspective during development.

9. **Reflecting on Outcomes:** Valuing each experience cultivates wisdom. Lessons advance strategies for greater responsibilities down the line.

By practicing leadership through authentic scenarios, adolescents can smoothly transition skills into adulthood. Focusing on process over product keeps goals engaging.

Case Studies

Tesla

In 2005, Tesla CEO Elon Musk convened a special task force to evaluate Tesla's product roadmap and recommend their first vehicle. Researchers analyzed battery capacity improvements and conducted global surveys, finding that consumers would pay a high price for an electric sports car experience.

The task force proposed a limited production run of the Tesla Roadster to test batteries and powertrain further. Musk invested $140 million in the prototype and manufacture of around 2,500 roadsters from 2008 to 2012. During this time, early owners provided critical unstructured feedback on the range, performance bugs, and charging infrastructure needs via online forums and surveys.

Engineers used this qualitative and quantitative user data to refine the Model S's drivetrain, battery cooling system, and software before its 2012 launch. Sales exceeded targets, validating Musk's strategy against naysayers. The Roadster's success raised $ 257 million, proving high-income environmentalists would adopt EVs.

Netflix

In 2010, Netflix faced stagnating growth and sought new opportunities. An international expansion task force analyzed internet speeds and device access in over 200 countries. Canada, the UK, and Latin America topped the list.

The task force then launched tailored Netflix experiences in these test markets. Canada received a limited catalog and price tiers to assess uptake. The UK piloted subtitle and dubbing options. Surveys tracked user satisfaction.

Two years of localization tweaking based on local feedback prepared Netflix for wider launches. For example, Latin America saw higher use of mobile phones, so the region launched mobile-first with localized payment options and lower pricing.

By systematically phasing expansion, Netflix seamlessly rolled out to over 190 countries by 2016. This research-driven process empowered well-informed decisions and rapid global growth.

Did You Know?

"82% of HR managers consider <u>leadership skills</u> a more important factor than GPA when reviewing candidates for college internships."

Chapter **6**

Juggle of Conflicts

As a leader, one must understand that conflicts within organizations or groups are inevitable and even beneficial if handled properly. Conflicts occur due to differences in perspectives, priorities, and personalities between individuals. Recognizing that conflicts will arise due to such natural divergences is an important part of being an effective leader. Leaders need to be able to identify conflicts in their early stages by actively listening to team members, being approachable, and being aware of undercurrents. Spotting conflicts early allows them to be addressed reasonably before escalating. It is also important for leaders to have a reasonable understanding of the root causes of conflicts. Understanding why conflicts occur helps leaders resolve issues by getting to the heart of disagreements in a fair-minded manner. This prevents conflicts from becoming personal attacks and makes it easier to find mutually agreeable solutions. By acknowledging conflicts as a natural part of any group and making an effort to comprehend different perspectives, leaders can facilitate reasonable discussions to negotiate solutions. This helps improve overall relationships, motivation, and productivity in the long run. A leader who is blind to conflicts or refuses to understand different viewpoints will find it challenging to build cohesion and address issues effectively.

It is crucial for effective leadership to recognize and understand conflicts from various angles. As individuals work together, differences in background, communication style, and priorities are inevitable. These divergences can easily lead to misunderstandings, bruised egos, and disagreements over approaches and deadlines. A wise leader acknowledges conflicts as a natural byproduct of collaboration between diverse team members. They make it a priority to actively look for signs of tensions developing, such as shortened interactions, offhand comments, or passive aggressiveness. Early intervention is key, so the leader checks in privately and objectively with those exhibiting friction to get all perspectives. Understanding root causes means asking thoughtful questions without accusations to bring hidden frustrations and misconceptions to light. The leader analyzes how personal biases or conflicting goals may unintentionally fuel tensions below the surface.

With various viewpoints gathered, the leader then facilitates a respectful discussion where all involved can voice concerns and validation. The goal is to find the underlying shared interests, not focus on assigning blame. Potential solutions are explored through flexible brainstorming so everyone feels their priorities are reasonably considered. Compromise that minimizes lingering resentments is key. If tensions still linger afterward, the leader follows up individually as needed and revisits the issue if more underlying issues surface. This approach diffuses power struggles and prevents conflicts from rupturing vital team relationships and motivation over the long haul.

Teenager's Edition

Establishing an environment conducive to effective conflict resolution is crucial for any leader. One strategy is implementing clear guidelines emphasizing respect, confidentiality, and cooperation during disputes. Mediation or one-on-one discussions should be encouraged over accusations to allow issues to surface calmly. Leaders can also set up anonymous feedback methods so minor conflicts are easier to detect and address before escalating. Training team members in active listening and assertive communication techniques gives them tools for airing issues constructively. Providing multiple outlets like peer mediation or an open-door policy shows conflicts will be handled fairly vs being punished.

Fostering psychological safety helps prevent conflicts from becoming too personal. Leaders accomplish this by role-modeling humility, taking responsibility for their own mistakes, and acknowledging no one is perfect. Team-building can help strengthen trust and bonds so conflicts are less likely to be seen as betrayals. Mediation practices like starting discussions by finding common ground and using "I feel" statements minimize defensiveness. Following up afterward to ensure perspectives are fully understood, and needs are reasonably accommodated provides closure.

Documenting resolutions demonstrates fairness. Surveying anonymously about conflict management gleans opportunities for improvement. And leaders who lead by example in constructively handling their own disputes command respect during team issues. With these proactive strategies, leaders cultivate an atmosphere where productive conflict is not feared but rather seen as a catalyst for positive change.

Conflict Resolution in the Global Market

Apple vs Samsung Electronics

For years, these tech titans were embroiled in over 30 lawsuits across 10 countries regarding patents for smartphone features. Through mediation, they analyzed each other's financial documents and sales strategies to better understand strategic motivations beyond legal filings. This revealed overlapping interests in mutually-beneficial partnerships versus zero-sum competition. They agreed to cross-license a portfolio of patents, allowing greater innovation through collaboration instead of taxation. Regular meetings established working relationships, building trust to cooperatively settle future issues.

Boeing vs Airbus

Trade representatives convened, sharing internal competitive analyses to get beyond rhetoric. Data illustrated the diverse costs each company faces, from labor rules to materials. With open dialog, nuances emerged - subsidies sometimes leveled playing fields versus solely benefiting one. By exploring flexible policy options, they crafted a nuanced agreement limiting certain subsidies but permitting others key to regional jobs. Review committees ensure cooperation continues, preventing backsliding into disputes.

Toyota vs. GM Canada

CEO mediations analyzed cultural factors like national pride and differing automotive histories. Toyota acknowledged nationalist passions in others' home markets, while GM recognized that global success requires respecting local tastes. They agreed to cooperative ventures for electric cars, sharing technology and facilities versus competing alone. Codes ensure fair competition and cooperation, preventing tensions from future "unfair practices" claims through regularly scheduled diplomacy.

These detailed resolutions show that granting opponents full humanity, sharing strategic insights beyond legalities, and crafting cooperative relationships - not just settlements - create sustainable, interest-based outcomes even in protracted global conflicts. Understanding multifaceted perspectives and mutual dependencies can forge voluntary win-win solutions where aggression and zero-sum stances risk perpetual disputes.

Chapter 7

Team + Leader = A Success Story

Developing a cohesive and high-performing team requires careful planning and effort. First, the leader must clearly define the team's purpose and goals to provide guidance and motivation. They then select individuals with complementary skills needed to accomplish tasks. Team building activities help members get acquainted, establish rapport, and learn one another's strengths. The leader fosters psychological safety so members are comfortable sharing ideas without judgment. Team norms and operating procedures are established to facilitate efficient collaboration. To function optimally, the team requires resources, training, and a collaborative work environment.

Teams need to be well-led because working in groups provides immense benefits. By combining diverse viewpoints and skills, teams can tackle complex problems and opportunities that no single individual could achieve alone. This allows for innovation and drives better solutions. However, without strong leadership, teams can become disorganized, unproductive due to infighting, or lack clear direction. The leader acts as the lynchpin, keeping members focused and accountable to goals. They motivate teamwork, resolve conflicts, ensure role clarity, and remove obstacles. A leader's communication, support, and ability to build consensus harness the power of the team for high performance.

Assembling the right group of individuals and developing them into a cohesive unit is crucial for success in modern organizations. However, teams require expert leadership and guidance to reach their full potential. A skilled leader is fundamental in coordinating efforts, maximizing strengths, and overcoming challenges to ensure a team delivers outstanding results.

Leadership plays a critical role in teams achieving high performance and success. As the team is first formed, the leader ensures each person's skills and strengths are assessed to compile the optimal configuration strategically. Comprehensive interviews identify personality fits and potential alignment issues. Through insight, the leader avoids groupthink and builds a cohesive unit with complementary talents.

Once established, the leader clearly defines the team's purpose and specific, measurable objectives. Regular check-ins assess progress and issues promptly. The leader assigns tasks based on ability but also rotates roles to broaden perspectives. Autonomy is provided with clear guardrails to boost ownership.

To facilitate cooperation, the leader emphasizes psychological safety through active listening and addressing tensions respectfully. Feedback is also constructive, not critical. Members are motivated by acknowledging even small wins. Morale and motivation are protected during setbacks through an emphasis on learning and adaptation.

Representation strengthens work quality and reputation. The leader markets achievements internally and fields issues neatly. Externally, they educate stakeholders on progress and needs. This gains resources and shields unfair treatment.

Leadership empowers calculated risk-taking through training and oversight. Failures are learning lessons, not punishments. Continuous development readies the team for greater responsibilities. Members thus feel truly valued and invested in shared success, working fluidly as an interdependent unit. Overall, a leader's strategic guidance and support maximizes team synergy far above any individual's limits.

Effective teams have diverse roles that work in harmony under a leader's guidance. Recognizing this, a leader maintains a growth mindset, understanding members may alternate or even change core roles over time as skills and priorities shift. Fixed thinking of roles could hamper potential. A follower role provides ideas to action-oriented initiators, while harmonizers mitigate tensions between fast-paced contributors and cautious thinkers. A leader acknowledges the value each brings and how roles naturally emerge from personal strengths. Their role is enabling this synergy versus mandating rigid labels.

Dynamics also depend on a leader's social intelligence. They understand some prefer collaborating while others recharge independently. Extroversion levels and communication styles vary among analytic debaters, empathetic supporters, and decisive directors. Rather than categorizing, the leader sees each person's humanity beyond surface traits. Trust is key to confidence in risking new roles. The leader expresses faith in members' potential through empowering initiatives and transparency about limitations to foster assurance without arrogance. They curb insular "in-groups" by actively engaging quieter voices and valuing diverse opinions equally.

Overall, a leader does not micro-manage roles or dynamics but instead facilitates an environment where varied talents align naturally. Flexibility, empathy, and confidence in others allow for optimal synergy as the team system freely self-organizes around a shared goal.

Teenager's Development to Be a Leader

- **Trust-fall exercises** - Having teenagers take turns falling back with eyes closed while others catch them builds trust and reliance on teammates. It teaches responsibility for others.

- **Communication challenges** - Activities like constructing a model together while facing away or retelling a story down the line improve listening skills and cooperation.

- **Debate competitions** - Structured debates on topics help teenagers learn to concisely make strong arguments, consider other perspectives, and draw logical conclusions.

- **Community service projects** - Planning and carrying out projects together, such as park cleanups, food drives, etc., fosters empathy, problem-solving, delegation of duties, and pride in accomplishments.

- **Outdoor adventures** - Experiences like hiking, camping, or ropes courses in small teams promote reliance on others, thinking on one's feet, and pushing personal boundaries.

- **Academic quiz bowls** - Preparing and competing as a unit to answer questions challenges teenagers to own strengths and contribute to a cohesive team dynamic centered around shared success.

- **Leadership seminars** - Focused classroom-style sessions teach teenagers public speaking, facilitation, and other skills for guiding future teams through projects and goals.

The most effective activities encourage responsibility, autonomy, flexibility, and collaboration towards a shared objective. This exposes teenagers to real leadership dynamics and strategies in a low-pressure setting.

Case Study 1

Google

At Google, employees are empowered to spend 20% of their time working on passion projects. This fosters innovation as engineers feel autonomy to explore ideas. It also builds trust in management that time isn't micromanaged. To encourage collaboration, open floor plans prioritize face-to-face interaction versus isolated desks. Free gourmet meals and on-site services create an enjoyable workplace where people naturally congregate and bond. As a result, employees are highly engaged and invested in the company's success, unleashing creativity.

Meanwhile, a traditional engineering firm faced quality issues after several failed projects. Employees complained of unrealistic deadlines and lack of input in decisions. The new CEO instituted an open-door policy, regularly soliciting anonymous feedback and addressing even minor complaints. Teams were given autonomy in work plans but clear responsibilities. Performance reviews emphasized learning over blame. Despite initial skepticism, survey data showed improvement in workplace satisfaction, stress, and work product after 6 months. Morale increased as employees felt heard, trusted as professionals, and invested in continuous growth. This renewed culture of psychological safety and accountability led to on-time deliverables meeting specifications. Profits grew as client satisfaction and retention rose.

These case studies demonstrate how fostering autonomy, collaboration, trust, and care for people's well-being and growth directly impacts team performance, satisfaction, retention, and, ultimately, business results. A supportive culture where employees feel valued and empowered to do their best work unleashes creativity and dedication.

Case Study 2

Netflix

At Netflix, the company is known for its strong culture of autonomy, transparency, and innovation. This culture has helped it succeed against larger competitors. In meetings, there are no formal presentations or PowerPoint decks - just candid conversations. Employees are empowered to cancel projects and make decisions without hierarchical approval as long as they can justify it.

Compensation is transparent, with all salaries published internally, so people are paid fairly relative to their contributions. There are no annual reviews either - just frequent feedback to keep employees improving. To foster collaboration, the Netflix campus has NO assigned seating. Open floor plans and food courts encourage serendipitous interactions. Senior leaders are also visible, roaming the offices to be easily approachable.

When the pandemic hit, Netflix nimbly transitioned to remote work due to existing practices of transparency, independence, and trust in employees. Productivity was maintained as people had the flexibility to work from anywhere. Netflix's unique culture has helped attract and retain top talent in highly competitive tech. It has seen continued success in developing original award-winning content, all while nimbly reacting to disruptions like COVID-19. This real case study highlights the power of empowerment, transparency, and autonomy in building high-performing, innovative teams.

Chapter **8**

A Leader's Wrist Watch

In the realm of professional pursuits, the art of managing time holds immense significance for every individual. As a leader, the weight of responsibility rests heavily upon your shoulders, requiring not only adeptness in overseeing projects, managing teams, and making critical decisions but also a keen mastery of time. In this chapter, we embark on a journey to unravel the importance of tailored time management strategies for effective leadership.

From the skill of discerning priorities amidst a flurry of tasks to the judicious delegation of responsibilities, and from fostering a culture of productivity within your team to safeguarding your own well-being and work-life balance, each aspect is meticulously explored. By equipping you with the necessary tools and insights to navigate the complexities of leadership with grace and efficacy, this chapter serves as a guiding light toward sustained success and fulfillment in your professional journey.

Secondly, time management plays a vital role in fostering effective communication and collaboration within teams. Leaders must allocate time for regular meetings, brainstorming sessions, and feedback discussions to keep team members aligned and motivated. By organizing and prioritizing these interactions, leaders can create an environment conducive to open communication, idea exchange, and problem-solving, ultimately leading to increased team productivity and cohesiveness.

First and foremost, effective time management is crucial for leaders to ensure the successful execution of projects and initiatives. Leaders often have the responsibility of overseeing multiple projects simultaneously, each with its own set of deadlines and deliverables. By managing their time efficiently, leaders can allocate resources effectively, delegate tasks appropriately, and monitor progress to ensure timely and budget-friendly completion of projects.

Furthermore, time management enables leaders to make informed and timely decisions in response to changing circumstances or unforeseen challenges. Throughout the day, leaders face a barrage of decisions, ranging from minor operational issues to major strategic choices. By effectively managing their time, leaders can allocate sufficient time for analysis, reflection, and consultation, ensuring that decisions are well-informed and aligned with organizational objectives.

Starting with a clear definition of time management and its significance, it refers to the ability to effectively allocate and prioritize one's time to accomplish tasks, meet deadlines, and achieve goals. It involves consciously organizing, planning, and controlling the time spent on specific activities to enhance productivity and efficiency. In the context of leadership, time management becomes even more critical due to the multifaceted responsibilities and demands placed on leaders.

In addition, the art of effective time management is crucial for leaders to uphold a harmonious equilibrium between their professional and personal lives, safeguarding against burnout. Leadership positions inherently demand a delicate balance between work duties, personal obligations, and self-preservation. Through strategic prioritization, establishing boundaries, and allocating time for relaxation and self-renewal, leaders can evade the perils of excessive workload and fatigue, thus ensuring sustained performance and overall well-being. By honing their time management skills, leaders can confidently navigate the intricacies of their roles with precision, ultimately propelling both organizational success and personal gratification.

When it comes to the development of effective leaders, it is important to incorporate idealistic values. Key to this development is the nurturing of integrity, honesty, and authenticity. Leaders who embody these values have the ability to inspire trust and respect within their teams, creating an environment of transparency and ethical behavior. Upholding integrity means that leaders remain steadfast in their principles, even in the face of challenges, which in turn earns them credibility and trust from their followers. Similarly, honesty encourages open communication and establishes a culture of accountability, where mistakes are acknowledged, learned from, and utilized as opportunities for personal and professional growth. Authenticity, on the other hand, empowers leaders to stay true to themselves and their values, forging genuine connections with their teams and fostering loyalty and commitment.

In contrast, the embodiment of compassion and empathy holds great significance in the cultivation of effective leadership. Exemplary leaders exhibit a profound sense of compassion by extending empathy and comprehension toward their team members, and acknowledging their individual strengths, obstacles, and aspirations. By nurturing a culture steeped in compassion and empathy, these leaders establish an environment that is both supportive and inclusive, ensuring that team members are not only valued but also earnestly heard, thus empowering them to contribute their utmost potential. Furthermore, the practice of compassionate leadership fosters a spirit of collaboration, cooperation, and collective problem-solving, resulting in heightened team performance and unity. Through the lens of empathy, leaders are able to proactively anticipate and address the needs and concerns of their team members, cultivating a profound sense of belonging and overall well-being.

A culture centered on goal-setting is an indispensable aspect of effective leadership. Goal-setting bestows leaders and their teams with a sense of direction and purpose, effectively guiding their endeavors toward the attainment of desired outcomes. Leaders who establish goals that are both ambitious and attainable inspire a profound sense of motivation and concentration among their teams, compelling them to venture beyond their comfort zones and strive for greatness. Additionally, goal-setting cultivates harmonization and accountability, ensuring that all individuals are tirelessly working towards a shared vision and wholeheartedly assuming ownership of their respective responsibilities. By consistently evaluating progress and adapting goals as necessary, leaders can adeptly navigate through ever-changing circumstances and steadfastly march toward triumph.

To develop into effective leaders, it is imperative to embrace idealistic principles such as integrity, honesty, compassion, and empathy. These values play a crucial role in shaping the character and moral compass of leaders, ultimately guiding them toward success. When coupled with a culture of setting goals, these values create a solid framework for leaders to build trust, encourage teamwork, and propel their organizations toward prosperity. By embodying these values and fostering a goal-oriented environment, leaders can cultivate a positive and impactful atmosphere where individuals flourish, teams succeed, and objectives are met.

Leader VS Boss: Battle of Leadership

The distinctions between a boss and a leader may appear subtle, but they are discernible, underscored by unique narratives and approaches. A boss tends to confine their responsibilities to overseeing employees, prioritizing task delegation, and adhering to predetermined guidelines. Conversely, a leader transcends conventional management, assuming the role of an inspiring and innovative figure who constantly motivates and fosters the growth of their team members.

A true leader distinguishes themselves by embracing a mentality of growth and adaptability, prioritizing the empowerment and development of their team members above all else. Unlike a boss who may rely on authority and rigidity, a leader remains open-minded and constantly seeks innovative solutions to drive efficiency and success for the collective. Their selfless approach fosters a culture of collaboration and continuous improvement, ultimately leading to the achievement of shared goals and aspirations.

Moreover, the difference between a boss and a leader is clearly demonstrated in how they approach collaboration and decision-making. A boss typically takes a commanding, hierarchical approach by giving orders, setting deadlines, and making decisions without consulting their team. This authoritative behavior can create a sense of powerlessness and isolation among employees, who may feel like insignificant parts of the company.

An exemplary leader nurtures an environment of cooperation, harmoniously collaborating with their team to accomplish common objectives. They foster authentic connections built on trust and admiration, actively engaging in daily activities and displaying a readiness to actively participate in the collective endeavor.

Furthermore, the discernible distinction between a boss and a leader becomes strikingly clear when faced with adversity and failure. In the face of setbacks or inadequacies, a leader embodies responsibility, taking full ownership of the situation and recognizing prospects for growth and enhancement. They perceive failure as an invaluable learning experience, contemplating what went awry and utilizing those insights to refine their approach. Conversely, a boss may gravitate towards deflecting blame onto others, evading accountability, and fostering a culture of scapegoating and finger-pointing. Rather than embracing responsibility, they may resort to exerting undue pressure on their subordinates, intensifying tensions and undermining team morale.

Finally, the distinction between a boss and a leader can be found in their commitment to fostering personal connections and the welfare of their team members. Unlike a boss who may exhibit an aloof and detached demeanor, solely focused on the execution of job responsibilities, a leader dedicates their time and energy to cultivating profound relationships with their team. They prioritize the cultivation of trust and camaraderie, acknowledging that robust interpersonal ties serve as the bedrock for both team unity and triumph.

By getting to know each team member individually, a leader gains valuable insights into their strengths, weaknesses, and motivations, enabling them to tailor their leadership style and approach accordingly. Unfortunately, the differences between a boss and a leader extend beyond superficial distinctions; anyone can witness their distinct fundamentals in mindset, methodology, and mission. While a boss may wield authority and control, a leader embodies inspiration, collaboration, accountability, and empathy, forging a path toward collective growth, success, and fulfillment.

Time Management Training: Prioritization Techniques

- **Eisenhower Matrix:** Introducing an exquisite time management tool bearing the prestigious name of former U.S. President Dwight D. Eisenhower. This unparalleled creation aims to assist you in seamlessly categorizing your tasks into distinct priority levels, meticulously derived from their utmost significance and exigency. Impeccably structured as a refined 2-by-2 matrix, this masterpiece showcases four quadrants, each meticulously tailored to elevate your productivity and efficiency;

- **Urgent and important:** Tasks that require immediate attention, such as addressing a pressing issue with a client or finalizing a project before a deadline.

- **Important, but not urgent:** Tasks that contribute to long-term goals, like strategic planning, employee development, and relationship-building.

- **Urgent but not important:** Tasks that demand immediate attention but don't contribute significantly to your long-term goals, such as responding to emails or attending to administrative tasks.

- **Neither urgent nor important:** Tasks that have little to no impact on your goals, like browsing social media or engaging in office gossip.

By utilizing this sophisticated prioritization technique, you will effortlessly streamline your tasks and maximize your time and energy. This method ensures that you focus your attention on important and time-sensitive tasks, preventing wasted effort on less crucial matters.

The Pareto Principle (80/20 Rule): The Pareto Principle, a captivating addition to one's repertoire of time management strategies, offers a distinct and intriguing approach. This principle asserts that by focusing our efforts on a mere 20 percent of our tasks, we can accomplish an astounding 80 percent of our objectives. Utilizing this perspective as a time management technique allows us to efficiently complete vital tasks with minimal exertion, subsequently enabling us to allocate our remaining 80 percent of tasks and tackle them simultaneously.

Bonus Learning Experience

In the pursuit of leadership, it is imperative for young individuals to surmount the hindrance of procrastination, as it serves as a vital milestone toward the fulfillment of their aspirations and the unlocking of their inherent capabilities. To facilitate this transformative journey, presented herein is a set of supplementary suggestions meticulously curated to empower teenagers in conquering the formidable adversary of procrastination and nurturing the indispensable qualities of effective leadership.

To begin, it is essential to establish precise and attainable goals known as SMART goals. By breaking down your overarching ambitions into smaller, feasible tasks with set deadlines, you can create a structured plan that offers guidance and inspiration. This strategic approach not only helps combat procrastination but also enables you to focus on your key priorities.

Furthermore, it is essential to organize your tasks according to their significance and immediacy. Consider utilizing frameworks such as the Eisenhower Matrix or The Pareto Principle to determine which tasks will have the most impact on your leadership journey. By focusing on the most critical tasks first, you can ensure that they receive the attention they deserve and avoid getting sidetracked by less important activities, ultimately reducing the tendency to delay important tasks.

Embracing a growth mindset and viewing setbacks as opportunities for growth is key to developing resilience and perseverance. By reframing failure as a stepping stone towards success, you can bounce back from challenges and continue to progress towards your goals.

Finally, it is essential to seek guidance and encouragement from mentors, peers, or loved ones who align with your goals and values. Surrounding yourself with positive influences who inspire and motivate you will help you stay focused on reaching your objectives. Sharing your successes and setbacks with others will create a sense of accountability and mutual support, reinforcing your dedication to overcoming procrastination and realizing your leadership ambitions. In summary, by incorporating these additional strategies, teenagers aspiring to become leaders can conquer procrastination, develop essential leadership skills, and set themselves up for success in their pursuits.

With dedication to setting clear objectives, prioritizing tasks, maintaining a structured routine, minimizing interruptions, embracing setbacks, and seeking guidance and accountability, adolescents can cultivate the discipline, resilience, and concentration necessary to unlock their leadership capabilities and contribute meaningfully to their communities and beyond.

Chapter **9**

A Day in the Life of a Leader

Behaviors and routines hold immense power in molding the conduct and impact of a leader. These consistent actions, ingrained in daily practice, not only shape decision-making and communication tactics but also define the overall efficacy of leadership.

Let's further explore the pivotal habits that pave the path to prosperous leadership:

Continuous Learning: Leaders who value continuous learning recognize that their success is not solely determined by their current knowledge but also by their commitment to expanding their expertise. They actively seek out new information and diverse perspectives from a variety of sources. One of the ways they achieve this is through regular reading, immersing themselves in a wide range of literature relevant to their field. Whether it be books on leadership principles, articles on industry developments, or case studies of thriving organizations, leaders understand the importance of staying informed and open to new ideas.

Furthermore, successful leaders must engage in seminars, workshops, and conferences to remain abreast of the most recent advancements within their industry. These gatherings offer invaluable chances to glean wisdom from industry experts, partake in meaningful discussions with colleagues, and acquire insights into emerging trends and best practices. By actively participating in such events, leaders not only enhance their knowledge base but also establish a network of contacts and resources that can bolster their ongoing personal and professional development. Seeking mentorship also plays a pivotal role in the continuous learning journey of leaders, as mentors can provide invaluable guidance, advice, and support rooted in their wealth of experiences and expertise.

Distinguished leaders recognize the significance of proactively seeking mentors who possess invaluable wisdom and unique perspectives. They comprehend the profound benefits of acquiring guidance from those who have traversed similar paths and are committed to devoting their time and energy to nurturing these invaluable connections.

Moreover, leaders must remain well-versed in industry trends, best practices, and emerging technologies to excel in their roles. Leaders must consistently stay informed about the latest advancements within their field, whether through industry literature, online platforms, or networking opportunities. By staying abreast of developments, leaders can proactively anticipate shifts, recognize potential opportunities, and make well-informed decisions that strategically position their organizations for success in a dynamic and ever-changing environment.

Clear Communication: Effective leaders recognize that clear communication is essential to their success. They understand that the way they communicate with their teams shapes the foundation of trust, alignment, and collaboration within their organization. By focusing on clear and concise communication, leaders cultivate an environment where team members feel appreciated, heard, and inspired to work towards shared objectives.

Active listening is a crucial component of effective communication for leaders. Successful leaders prioritize attentively listening to their team members to gain insight into their viewpoints, worries, and suggestions. Through exhibiting empathy and showing respect through active listening, leaders cultivate an inclusive and encouraging atmosphere where all opinions are acknowledged and appreciated.

In addition, astute leaders understand the significance of imparting constructive feedback as an integral component of their communication approach. They consistently and courteously offer feedback, directing their attention toward particular actions or results rather than individual traits. Through the art of constructive feedback, these leaders assist their team members in pinpointing areas for enhancement, gaining wisdom from past encounters, and advancing their professional aptitude.

In addition, successful leaders must establish a foundation of clear communication within their team or organization. This involves effectively conveying the goals, objectives, and expectations consistently and articulately. By communicating the organization's vision, mission, and values compellingly, leaders can foster a sense of unity and dedication among team members.

Effective leaders utilize a variety of communication channels, including written communication and non-verbal cues, to enhance the effectiveness of their verbal messages. By incorporating emails, memos, and other written tools, they provide additional clarity and context to their verbal communications. Furthermore, they attentively observe non-verbal cues like body language and facial expressions to assess comprehension and interest during interactions.

Emotional Intelligence: Emotional intelligence (EI) emerges as an indispensable foundation of impactful leadership, underscoring the significance of comprehending and handling emotions in both personal and interpersonal contexts. Leaders who possess elevated EI possess a remarkable capacity to skillfully navigate the intricate realm of human emotions within the organizational setting. They consistently strive to acknowledge and regulate their own emotional states, a critical undertaking for preserving poise and maintaining mental acuity, particularly in demanding or stressful circumstances. By attaining mastery over their emotional reactions, these leaders can make judicious decisions and adeptly guide their teams through adversity, instilling confidence and fortitude in their followers.

Furthermore, leaders who possess a remarkable level of emotional intelligence go beyond simply being aware of their own emotions and being able to control them. They go the extra mile to truly comprehend the emotions and viewpoints of their team members, thus nurturing a culture of empathy and utmost respect throughout the organization. By actively listening and genuinely empathizing with others, these leaders establish an atmosphere where individuals feel a profound sense of worth, encouragement, and comprehension. By acknowledging and validating the emotions of others, they establish trust and rapport, which are imperative for fostering resilient and harmonious teams.

In addition, leaders who possess strong emotional intelligence are essential in influencing the overall culture of the organization. They consistently exhibit emotionally intelligent traits such as authenticity, humility, and vulnerability in their interactions with others, serving as a role model for their team. By promoting these behaviors, they inspire team members to enhance their own emotional intelligence, ultimately leading to a more collaborative and efficient work atmosphere. Furthermore, these leaders actively foster an environment of psychological safety, where individuals feel empowered to freely share their thoughts, ideas, and worries without facing criticism or backlash.

Strategic Thinking: Leaders with exceptional strategic thinking abilities have a consistent practice of looking beyond the present obstacles and concentrating on the broader perspective. They engage in a thorough examination of both internal and external influences affecting their organization, striving to comprehend market dynamics, competitive pressures, and upcoming developments. By embracing a strategic outlook, these leaders are more prepared to foresee shifts, recognize possibilities, and manage potential threats, ultimately positioning their organizations for enduring progress and a competitive edge.

Furthermore, strategic thinking entails aligning actions with the overarching vision and goals of the organization. Successful leaders prioritize the communication of a clear and compelling vision that inspires and motivates their team members. They ensure that each individual comprehends the strategic objectives and their specific role in achieving them, fostering a sense of purpose and unity throughout the organization. Through this alignment of individual efforts with the broader strategic direction, these leaders create synergy and coherence, enabling their organizations to progress with clarity and determination.

Furthermore, the art of strategic thinking entails a harmonious and ongoing journey of appraisal and fine-tuning. Exceptional leaders cultivate a practice of consistently scrutinizing and honing their strategies, taking into account the fluidity of circumstances and the invaluable insights provided by feedback. They possess a remarkable ability to remain nimble and flexible, ready to gracefully pivot and recalibrate their trajectory to ensure harmonious alignment with the aspirations and objectives of their organization. Embracing an ethos of perpetual improvement and knowledge acquisition, these visionary leaders nurture an atmosphere of ingenuity and fortitude, positioning their enterprises for enduring triumph amidst the ever-shifting terrain of the corporate world.

Empowering Others: The act of empowering others is a distinguishing characteristic of exceptional leadership, exemplifying a deep belief in the abilities and potential of team members. Rather than engaging in excessive control, prosperous leaders comprehend the importance of distributing authority and granting individuals the opportunity to assume responsibility for their tasks. They consistently assign duties in a manner that aligns with the unique skills, talents, and passions of each team member. By bestowing autonomy and decision-making power upon their colleagues, these leaders cultivate a sense of ownership and responsibility, which are indispensable in propelling performance and attaining the objectives of the organization.

In addition, exemplary leaders transcend the act of delegating tasks by offering continuous support and valuable resources to their team members. They prioritize the removal of any obstacles while providing invaluable guidance and offering coaching and mentorship whenever necessary. Through their unwavering support and encouragement, these leaders empower their team members to overcome obstacles, foster the development of new skills, and ultimately unlock their inherent potential. Furthermore, they cultivate an environment that fosters continuous learning and personal growth, wherein individuals are inspired to actively pursue opportunities for advancement and self-improvement, both within their personal lives and professional endeavors.

Moreover, accomplished leaders foster an atmosphere of responsibility among their teams, where individuals assume ownership of their actions and achievements. They establish unequivocal standards and benchmarks for triumph, ensuring that team members are held accountable for delivering tangible outcomes. Simultaneously, they create a nurturing environment that encourages individuals to fearlessly take chances, derive valuable lessons from setbacks, and evolve through their encounters. By nurturing a climate steeped in accountability and knowledge acquisition, these leaders embolden their team members to pioneer, explore uncharted territories, and surpass existing limitations, thereby propelling unceasing progress and ingenuity within the organization.

Leading by Example: Exemplifying the ideals of effective leadership, leading by example stands as a fundamental principle that underscores the imperative harmony between one's rhetoric and conduct. Astute leaders acknowledge their role as beacons of inspiration for their teams, fully aware that their actions wield a profound influence over the entire fabric of their organization's culture and performance. By embodying the values and principles they ardently advocate, these leaders effortlessly establish unwavering credibility and trust among their esteemed team members, thereby kindling a spark of aspiration within them to mirror similar commendable behaviors. Whether it involves showcasing unwavering integrity, fostering transparency, or making ethically sound decisions, these adept leaders consistently emphasize the significance of consistently leading by example, thereby setting an unparalleled standard of excellence for others to ardently embrace.

True leadership goes beyond mere words and requires leading by example. Successful leaders demonstrate the behavior they wish to see in others, consistently exhibiting qualities such as punctuality, reliability, and dedication to achieving outstanding outcomes. Through modeling a strong work ethic and a pursuit of excellence, leaders inspire their team members to take pride in their work and take accountability for their actions. By setting a positive precedent, leaders cultivate a culture of responsibility and success within the organization, motivating individuals to take ownership of their responsibilities and strive for continual growth.

Leading through personal example cultivates an atmosphere of trust and admiration within the organization. When leaders exhibit integrity, honesty, and transparency in their actions, they establish trust and credibility with their team members. This trust serves as the bedrock for strong, collaborative relationships, facilitating open communication, effective decision-making, and mutual support. Furthermore, by treating others with courtesy and grace, leaders establish a positive work environment that nurtures a sense of worth, appreciation, and empowerment among individuals, encouraging them to contribute their utmost. This culture of trust and respect not only elevates employee morale and engagement but also nurtures loyalty and retention, as individuals are more inclined to remain dedicated to an organization where they feel esteemed and honored.

Prioritization and Time Management: The mastery of prioritization and time management plays a vital role in the realm of effective leadership, particularly in the demanding and fast-paced landscape of today's business world. Exceptional leaders understand that they are consistently faced with an array of obligations and duties, all competing for their attention. In response to this challenge, they cultivate the invaluable skill of developing robust strategies for prioritization, allowing them to efficiently handle their workload and concentrate on matters of true significance. By establishing clear priorities, these leaders ensure that their valuable time and energy are devoted to high-impact tasks that directly align with the objectives and ambitions of their organization. This strategic approach not only optimizes productivity but also empowers leaders to make substantial and meaningful contributions toward propelling the organization forward.

Skilled leaders recognize the significance of concentrating on impactful tasks that bring the utmost value to the organization. They carefully select where to invest their time and resources, giving priority to activities that hold the potential for substantial results. By dedicating their efforts to tasks that are in line with strategic objectives and produce concrete outcomes, leaders can greatly influence the success of the organization. Furthermore, by entrusting less critical tasks to their team members or utilizing technology and automation where feasible, leaders can create space for focusing on important strategic initiatives and crucial decision-making processes.

The art of prioritizing and managing time is not merely an individual skill; it possesses a profound influence on the effectiveness and productivity of a team. Astute leaders understand the significance of communicating explicit priorities and expectations to their team members, fostering collective unity and shared objectives. Through the provision of lucidity and guidance, these leaders empower their teams to discern the importance of their tasks and distribute their time and resources judiciously. Furthermore, by fostering a culture centered around responsibility and performance-driven outcomes, these leaders cultivate an environment wherein individuals assume personal accountability for their work and consistently deliver exceptional results.

Building Relationships: At the core of successful leadership lies the art of cultivating relationships, which serves as the bedrock for fostering trust, promoting collaboration, and enhancing team unity. Leaders acknowledge that their success is intertwined with the strength of their connections with others, underscoring the importance of building meaningful relationships to drive organizational effectiveness and prosperity. Thus, adept leaders consistently prioritize nurturing these interpersonal bonds, understanding that they are crucial for cultivating a harmonious workplace culture and facilitating collective accomplishments.

Building strong relationships with team members is crucial for effective leadership. Taking the time to understand each individual's strengths, motivations, and goals shows genuine interest and empathy. This fosters a sense of camaraderie and mutual respect within the team, leading to better collaboration and communication. By creating a supportive work culture where everyone feels valued and understood, leaders can boost morale and engagement.

Skilled leaders demonstrate a deliberate commitment to expressing gratitude for the valuable contributions and achievements of their team members. They possess a deep understanding of the significance of acknowledgment and commendation in nurturing a harmonious work atmosphere and driving individuals to attain their utmost potential. Be it through spoken acclamation, written correspondence, or thoughtful acts of appreciation; these leaders guarantee their team members feel esteemed and recognized for their diligent endeavors. By acknowledging and celebrating triumphs, leaders fortify a milieu of distinction and inspire unwavering devotion and allegiance among their team members.

Successful leaders prioritize the establishment of a nurturing workplace atmosphere that promotes a sense of appreciation and dignity among all team members. They cultivate a culture of inclusivity that embraces a variety of viewpoints and empowers individuals to express their thoughts and beliefs. Through encouraging transparent communication and cooperation, leaders enable the advancement of fresh ideas and inventive solutions, propelling organizational advancement and achievement. Furthermore, by fostering an environment of emotional security, leaders cultivate a space where individuals are encouraged to take chances, embrace errors, and glean lessons from setbacks, ultimately enhancing the team's resilience and versatility.

Case Study

Satya Nadella – CEO of Microsoft

The tenure of Satya Nadella as CEO of Microsoft serves as a resounding testament to the immense power and potential of effective leadership. In the year 2014, Nadella took the helm of this renowned technology behemoth during a pivotal moment, confronted with the daunting obstacles of sluggish growth and an antiquated corporate environment. Nevertheless, through his poised composure and forward-thinking vision, he orchestrated an extraordinary transformation that revitalized the company's trajectory. This compelling case study delves deep into Nadella's remarkable voyage of transformative leadership at Microsoft, illuminating the strategic initiatives and profound outcomes that reshaped the very essence of the organization.

In the early 2010s, Microsoft faced a challenge of perception, as it was perceived as being outdated despite its industry dominance. Despite its struggles to innovate and keep pace with market changes, the company ventured into new markets, such as smartphones and tablets, with disappointing outcomes. Under Nadella's leadership, Microsoft underwent a revitalization and cultural transformation to stimulate innovation and drive growth.

Upon assuming leadership, Nadella quickly implemented a thorough overhaul of Microsoft's culture and strategic direction. At the core of this transformation was the establishment of a new mission to empower individuals and organizations worldwide to achieve greater success. This mission prioritized customer satisfaction and cooperation. Nadella also led a shift towards a more empathetic, inclusive, and collaborative work environment, fostering a culture of openness and innovation. Furthermore, he drove Microsoft's adoption of open-source and cloud technologies, recognizing their potential for fostering collaboration and driving innovation. Becoming a Platinum Member of the Linux Foundation and investing in cloud-based services like Azure were key steps in this transformative journey.

Under Nadella's visionary leadership, Microsoft achieved remarkable financial success, with stock prices soaring to nearly five times their previous peak. This growth was driven by the company's strategic transition to cloud-based services and increased collaboration with open-source technologies. Culturally, Microsoft underwent a significant transformation, creating a more inclusive and innovative work environment where employees were encouraged to take risks and drive innovation. This shift propelled Microsoft to the forefront of the technology industry, positioning the company as a leader in delivering cutting-edge solutions and outperforming competitors in a constantly changing market.

In summary, Satya Nadella's exceptional leadership at Microsoft provides a remarkable example of visionary leadership in practice. By implementing strategic initiatives centered on cultural change, customer focus, and innovation, Nadella successfully rejuvenated Microsoft's corporate culture and propelled its growth. As Microsoft flourishes under Nadella's guidance, his tenure exemplifies the profound impact of leadership in shaping the future of both organizations and industries.

Chapter 10

Self-Reflection

Identifying the characteristics of an individual leader requires observation, assessment, and understanding of which qualities are typically associated with effective leadership. Here are some steps to help you identify someone's leadership traits:

Observation: Watch how someone acts when they are with other people and how they make choices. See if they are helpful and how they deal with problems or arguments.

Communication Skills: Good leaders know how to talk and listen really well. They can explain things clearly and make others feel excited and motivated. They are also good at showing their feelings without using words.

Vision and Goal Orientation: A leader is like a captain of a ship. They know where they want to go, and they make plans to get there. They need to find people who think ahead, have good ideas, and are not afraid to try new things.

Empathy and Emotional Intelligence: True leaders are really good at understanding how other people feel and thinking about things from their point of view. Watch how they treat their team members, listen to their worries, and stay calm when things get tough.

Decision-Making Abilities: Leaders have to make hard choices when they are in a tough situation. They need to be able to look at all the information, think about different options, and make smart decisions that are best for everyone in their group or company.

Integrity and Ethics: Find people who always do the right thing and are good role models. Good leaders show others how to be honest and do the right thing, making other people trust and believe in them.

Resilience and Adaptability: Leadership means being a good leader even when things are hard or uncertain. Look for people who can stay strong and positive when faced with tough situations, can change their plans when things don't go as expected, and are willing to learn from their mistakes.

Collaboration and Team Building: Effective leaders work together with others to achieve a goal. They make sure everyone gets along and helps each other out. They build friendships, make people feel strong, and keep everyone united and working well together.

Initiative and Accountability: Leaders are people who take charge and are responsible for what they do and the results of their choices. They are the ones who actively look for ways to help, take control of their responsibilities, and make sure they do a good job.

Continuous Learning and Growth: True leaders are always trying to learn and get better at what they do. Look for people who are excited to learn new things, take advice well, and are always trying to improve themselves and help others. By looking for these qualities in someone, you can see if they would be a good leader in different situations. Remember, being a good leader can mean different things, and people may have different strengths in leadership.

Are You a Leader?

The truth is that leadership potential lies within all of us, waiting to be unleashed. The key to unlocking this potential lies in a powerful tool: self-reflection. By taking the time to examine our strengths, weaknesses, values, and motivations, we can gain valuable insights into our natural leadership tendencies. Through this process, we can embark on a path of continuous learning and growth, cultivating the qualities necessary to become effective and impactful leaders.

Go get a diary, answer the 20 questions, and analyze how good of a leader you are yet.

1. What are you proud of accomplishing recently?
2. Can you describe a time when you helped someone else?
3. What challenges have you faced recently, and how did you handle them?
4. What are your strengths, and how do you use them?
5. Are there areas where you feel you could improve, and how do you plan to do so?
6. What goals do you have for yourself, and what steps are you taking to achieve them?
7. How do you feel when you succeed at something challenging?
8. Have you experienced failure or setbacks recently, and what did you learn from them?

9. Are there any mistakes you've made that you wish you could correct, and what would you do differently?

10. How do you handle conflicts or disagreements with others?

11. What do you enjoy doing in your free time, and why?

12. Can you describe a time when you felt proud of yourself for standing up for what you believe in?

13. How do you take care of yourself, physically and emotionally?

14. Are there any activities or hobbies you'd like to try in the future?

15. What values are important to you, and how do you demonstrate them in your actions?

16. How do you feel about your relationships with friends and family members?

17. Are there any goals or dreams you have for the future, and what steps can you take to work towards them?

18. What do you think makes you unique or special?

19. How do you handle stress or difficult emotions?

What are you grateful for in your life right now?

Chapter **11**

EI is The New IQ

Emotional Intelligence (EI) is paramount for effective leadership across diverse contexts, as it encompasses a range of skills vital for guiding and inspiring others. Self-awareness is a fundamental component of Emotional Intelligence, allowing leaders to comprehend their emotions, motivations, and actions. This understanding empowers leaders to make intentional decisions that uphold their values and aspirations, cultivating authenticity and integrity in their leadership style. By acknowledging their emotional triggers and reactions, leaders can successfully control their conduct and remain composed, even amidst challenging circumstances.

Furthermore, Emotional Intelligence enables leaders to connect with their team members on a deeper level by understanding and acknowledging their emotions and perspectives. This fosters trust and strong bonds within the team, leading to a supportive work environment where individuals feel appreciated, heard, and inspired to excel. Empathetic leaders are able to communicate effectively by tailoring their messages to resonate with the emotions and experiences of their team members.

The art of effective communication is further elevated by the presence of emotional intelligence, becoming an essential skill for leaders. Those who possess a profound understanding of emotional intelligence actively engage in attentive listening, discern nonverbal cues and convey their thoughts with clarity and empathy. By fostering an environment that encourages open dialogue, team members are bestowed with a sense of validation, respect, and empowerment to freely express their ideas and concerns. In turn, this open channel of communication cultivates collaboration, innovation, and effective problem-solving within teams, ultimately propelling the organization toward success.

In the realm of leadership, conflict resolution is a crucial element, and emotional intelligence plays a pivotal role. Leaders who possess a high level of emotional intelligence gracefully navigate conflicts with tact and diplomacy, as they possess a profound understanding of the underlying emotions and perspectives of those involved. Instead of exacerbating tensions, they skillfully facilitate constructive dialogue, seek common ground, and strive for mutually beneficial resolutions. This extraordinary ability to effectively manage conflicts fosters a tranquil work environment where differences are embraced, celebrated, and resolved harmoniously.

Additionally, leaders who possess high emotional intelligence are adept at making informed decisions that blend emotional intuition with logical reasoning. They carefully evaluate the emotional consequences of their choices on both individuals and teams, in addition to the practical outcomes. By incorporating a variety of viewpoints and anticipating emotional responses, they are able to make decisions that uphold organizational values and objectives, cultivating a culture of trust and assurance among their followers.

Furthermore, leaders who possess a deep understanding of emotions have the exceptional ability to ignite inspiration and propel their teams forward by nurturing a harmonious and all-encompassing environment. They possess the astuteness to acknowledge and honor the unique contributions of individuals, impart invaluable feedback, and foster a profound sense of unity and significance within the organization. This instills unwavering loyalty, unwavering dedication, and exceptional achievements among team members, thereby propelling the organization toward triumph and unwavering fortitude in the face of adversity.

Understanding IQ and EI: Choosing One

In an era marked by modesty and rapid change, where uncertainties and interconnectedness reign supreme, the justification of Intelligence Quotient (IQ) and Emotional Intelligence (EI) becomes profoundly significant. While IQ traditionally gauges cognitive prowess in areas such as logical reasoning and problem-solving. All of these are essential for navigating intricate dilemmas; the importance of EI in today's world cannot be underestimated. As collaboration, adaptability, and interpersonal skills become increasingly vital, EI emerges as a crucial asset in facing the complexities of our modern landscape.

While intelligence quotient (IQ) may equip individuals with the intellectual capacity to solve complex problems and adjust to changing situations, emotional intelligence (EI) provides a unique array of equally essential abilities, if not more significant, particularly in times of modesty. EI encompasses the aptitude to identify, comprehend, regulate, and communicate emotions within oneself and others. It empowers individuals to forge deep connections, maneuver through social intricacies, and motivate others toward shared objectives. In an era dominated by the importance of collaboration, empathy, and the ability to bounce back, EI emerges as a pivotal element for achieving success.

In the domain of leadership, a strong intellect can certainly aid in making strategic decisions and solving complex problems. However, true effectiveness in leadership is often dependent on the capacity to forge emotional connections with others. Leaders possessing high emotional intelligence are able to instill trust, promote teamwork, and handle conflicts with poise and understanding. They recognize the significance of creating a welcoming environment where every individual feels appreciated and encouraged to give their utmost.

Furthermore, during these humble moments marked by escalated pressures and intricate human dynamics, emotional intelligence assumes a paramount significance in terms of individual welfare and psychological well-being. Those possessing elevated levels of emotional intelligence possess the ability to handle stress proficiently, foster harmonious connections, and nurture a formidable fortitude when confronted with hardship. This profound emotional resilience not only enriches the entirety of one's existence but also serves as a catalyst for prolonged achievements and profound contentment.

It is of utmost importance to acknowledge that intelligence quotient (IQ) and emotional intelligence (EI) are not in opposition, but rather, they harmoniously enhance one another. While IQ may confer an advantageous position in specific realms, the attainment of long-lasting triumph and contentment often necessitates a harmonious blend of cognitive aptitude and emotional proficiency. Embracing both IQ and EI as mutually reinforcing virtues empowers individuals to gracefully navigate the complexities presented during challenging periods with unwavering resilience, adaptability, and a deep sense of empathy.

In summary, it is evident that while IQ holds significance in tasks demanding analytical thinking and specialized knowledge, Emotional Intelligence emerges as equally indispensable, if not more so, in our contemporary, interconnected, and ever-evolving society. By acknowledging the significance of both cognitive and emotional capabilities, individuals can nurture a comprehensive skill set that empowers them to flourish amidst the intricacies of the present era, thereby fostering personal development, achieving professional triumph, and attaining overall contentment.

Significance of Empathetic and Sympathetic Factors

The essential qualities of empathy and sympathy in leadership are paramount for teenagers as they navigate the crucial period of their formative years. These attributes enable young leaders to establish profound connections with their peers, promoting a sense of understanding, solidarity, and cohesion within their communities.

Empathy, the profound capacity to comprehend and resonate with the emotions of others, is an essential trait for adolescent leaders to nurture. By demonstrating empathy towards their peers, young leaders can appreciate and validate the various experiences and sentiments that their peers encounter. Be it navigating academic stressors, familial obstacles, or individual trials, empathetic leaders establish a comforting and inclusive atmosphere where everyone is understood and appreciated.

In addition, the virtue of sympathy enhances the empathetic nature of teenage leaders, enabling them to exhibit genuine care and understanding towards their peers' welfare. These compassionate leaders engage in active listening, providing solace, motivation, and practical support as necessary. Through the expression of sympathy, youthful leaders have the opportunity to cultivate trust and connection with their peers, fostering a harmonious and united spirit within their communities.

By integrating empathetic and sympathetic elements into their leadership style, adolescents have the power to ignite a wave of favorable transformation and foster an atmosphere of inclusiveness. Instead of fixating solely on personal aspirations or goals, these compassionate leaders prioritize the overall well-being and contentment of their comrades. By exemplifying acts of benevolence, empathy, and encouragement, teenage leaders have the ability to cultivate a culture steeped in empathy and sympathy, empowering all individuals to flourish and triumph in unison.

It is crucial for teenagers to embrace and embody the compassionate and understanding facets of leadership in order to skillfully maneuver the trials of adolescence and foster robust, enduring communities. Through showcasing empathy and sympathy, youthful leaders have the power to profoundly impact the lives of their peers and ignite a hopeful, more empathetic tomorrow for future generations.

Developing Emotional Intelligence Skills

- **Journaling:** Encourage teenagers to regularly write about their thoughts, feelings, and experiences. This helps them develop self-awareness and reflection.

- **Role-playing:** Engage in role-playing scenarios to help teens understand different emotions and perspectives, building empathy and social awareness.

- **Mindfulness exercises:** Practice techniques like deep breathing, meditation, and body scans to help teenagers regulate their emotions and manage stress effectively.

- **Group discussions:** Facilitate group discussions on topics related to emotions, empathy, and communication to encourage teens to express themselves and understand others better.

- **Empathy-building activities:** Engage in activities like volunteering, community service projects, or visiting nursing homes to foster empathy and compassion towards others.

- **Identifying emotions:** Use tools like emotion cards or mood meters to help teenagers identify and label their emotions accurately, promoting emotional literacy.

- **Conflict resolution workshops:** Teach teenagers strategies for resolving conflicts peacefully, such as active listening, compromise, and finding win-win solutions.

- **Emotional regulation games:** Play games that require emotional regulation, such as "Emotion Charades" or "Feelings Bingo," to help teens practice managing their emotions in different situations.

- **Creative expression:** Encourage teens to express their emotions through art, music, writing, or other creative outlets, fostering emotional exploration and self-expression.

- **Reflective exercises:** Provide prompts for teenagers to reflect on past experiences, challenges, and successes, helping them learn from their emotions and develop resilience.

Chapter **12**

Be an Ethical Leader

Ethical leadership embodies a refined and compelling approach that places a premium on the values of integrity, honesty, fairness, and responsibility in the realms of decision-making and behavior. Ethical leaders not only exemplify moral principles themselves but also cultivate a culture of ethics within their teams, inspiring and motivating individuals to uphold similar standards. By setting a sterling example and consistently demonstrating ethical conduct, they foster a climate of accountability where both themselves and others are held to the highest ethical standards.

The significance of ethical leadership is found in its capacity to cultivate trust, admiration, and authenticity within both organizational and communal settings. By upholding ethical standards, leaders lay the groundwork for a culture rooted in honesty and openness, ultimately fostering a sense of unity and commitment among employees. Furthermore, ethical leadership facilitates the development of robust connections with various stakeholders, such as clients, shareholders, and the general public, resulting in heightened levels of confidence and allegiance.

The realm of ethical leadership extends across a multitude of domains concerning decision-making and conduct within an establishment. It entails the conscientious selection of morally upright options pertaining to the treatment of employees, equitable allocation of resources, fulfillment of corporate social obligations, and adherence to legal statutes and regulations. Ethical leaders possess the sagacity to contemplate the repercussions of their choices on all stakeholders, prioritizing the welfare of the collective over immediate financial gains or personal advantages.

Moreover, ethical leadership elevates the stature and brand image of an organization, engendering heightened customer loyalty and fostering a positive perception among the general public. By championing ethical conduct, these leaders also play a vital role in shaping a more virtuous society and making significant contributions to the greater good.

Embracing ethical leadership not only aligns with moral principles but also presents a strategic advantage by fostering a positive cycle of trust, cooperation, and achievements within both organizational and community settings. The dynamic of mentorship in leadership development is a potent relationship in which a seasoned mentor provides guidance and support to a less experienced mentee, aiding in their growth and development as effective leaders. This form of mentorship is a crucial foundation for leadership advancement, offering invaluable support, insight, and motivation to emerging leaders as they progress in their careers and strive for excellence.

Mentorship: A Key Component in Leadership Development

A crucial element in the cultivation of leadership lies within the realm of mentorship. It entails the graceful transmission of knowledge, skills, and profound insights from the mentor to the mentee. Mentors, being custodians of their own invaluable experiences and expertise, graciously bestow practical advice, impart wisdom gleaned from lessons learned, and offer unique perspectives that aid in the mentee's development of their own leadership skills. This transfer of knowledge is skillfully tailored to suit the individual needs and aspirations of the mentee, thus facilitating bespoke guidance and unwavering support.

Remember, mentorship goes beyond simply sharing information; it is about nurturing mentees' personal growth and self-awareness. Mentors exemplify leadership qualities like integrity, empathy, resilience, and strategic thinking, serving as guides for mentees to learn and emulate. Through this mentorship, mentees can enhance their understanding of effective leadership and refine their own leadership approach and beliefs.

The guidance and support provided through mentorship in leadership development create a conducive and empowering space for mentees to discover and enhance their capabilities. Mentors provide valuable feedback, inspiration, and encouragement, aiding mentees in overcoming obstacles, boosting self-assurance, and unlocking their full potential. This invaluable mentorship can be especially advantageous for up-and-coming leaders navigating the complexities and uncertainties of advancing in their professional journeys.

Mentorship for leadership development extends beyond individual mentor-mentee relationships to encompass group mentorship initiatives. These programs facilitate peer learning, networking, and collaboration, providing mentees with a diverse range of leadership perspectives and experiences. Similarly, ethical leadership acts as a moral compass guiding leaders towards integrity, honesty, and accountability in their decision-making processes, prioritizing the well-being of stakeholders and the greater good.

Ultimately, ethical leaders establish precise guidelines for conduct within their organizations, encouraging a climate where honesty is esteemed and acknowledged. They ensure that both themselves and their team members adhere to these guidelines and swiftly address any unethical behavior. Ethical leadership transcends the confines of the organization, as leaders acknowledge their duty to society and prioritize endeavors that benefit the greater good. By constantly seeking to enhance their ethical decision-making abilities through ongoing education and introspection, ethical leaders aim to instill trust and credibility among their followers.

BONUS TIPS

Navigating the intricate landscape of ethical dilemmas is an imperative pursuit, one that resonates deeply within our personal and professional realms. Allow me to present to you a collection of invaluable bonus tips, meticulously curated to guide you toward elegant resolutions that uphold the highest ethical standards:

Consider the Consequences: Before embarking on a course of action, indulge in a thoughtful contemplation of the potential consequences that may occur. Delve beyond the immediate aftermath and delve into the profound long-term implications that may affect the numerous individuals vested in the matter. By meticulously examining the outcomes, you shall be empowered to forge decisions congruent with moral values and reduce any potential detriment inflicted upon others.

Seek Different Perspectives: Engage in fruitful consultations with esteemed peers to assimilate a multitude of perspectives pertaining to the current circumstance. Deliberating conscientiously upon the ethical quandary alongside esteemed colleagues, experienced mentors, or trusted confidants shall bestow upon your invaluable insights, heretofore disregarded. This meticulous process shall enable you to discern hidden deficiencies and consequently arrive at a judicious resolution fortified by comprehensive knowledge.

Adhere to Core Values: Take a moment to contemplate your personal and organizational values, allowing them to gracefully steer your decision-making journey. Unearth the underlying principles that hold the utmost importance to you, and let these values harmoniously guide your every action. Embracing integrity and honesty shall function as a guiding light, illuminating the path to navigate even the most arduous ethical dilemmas.

Evaluate Intentions: Reflect on the motivations driving your actions and determine if they stem from a desire for personal gain or a sincere commitment to ethical principles. Assess whether your intentions adhere to moral standards and if you are placing the well-being of others above your own interests.

Assess Legal and Ethical Standards: Immerse yourself in a comprehensive understanding of the laws, regulations, and ethical principles that pertain to the present circumstances. Assure that your choices align with both legal mandates and the ethical standards dictated by esteemed codes of professional conduct or organizational policies. Nevertheless, acknowledge that mere legality should not be conflated with righteousness, as ethical deliberations may transcend mere legal obligations.

Practice Empathy and Compassion: By stepping into the shoes of those impacted by your choices, you can better understand their viewpoints and emotions. Developing empathy and compassion will guide you in making decisions that show care and consideration for others. Aim to find a harmonious balance between different interests while prioritizing minimizing harm and ensuring fairness.

Be Transparent and Accountable: Ensure that your decision-making process is characterized by utmost transparency, enabling you to artfully justify your actions to pertinent stakeholders. Embrace the nobility of acknowledging any potential conflicts of interest and gracefully assume responsibility for the outcomes of your decisions. Cultivate an organizational ethos that reveres and upholds ethical conduct, fostering a sense of accountability among all members. By seamlessly integrating these invaluable suggestions into your decision-making approach, you will deftly navigate ethical dilemmas with enhanced poise and integrity, thereby contributing to an environment that epitomizes ethical and socially responsible practices.

Chapter **13**

Secret Recipe of Leadership

Step into the enchanting voyage through the elaborate realm of leadership, where we delve profoundly into the very essence of genuine guidance adorned with integrity, bravery, and discernment. Within this captivating chapter, we embark upon a noble quest to decipher the fundamental principles that form the foundation of influential leadership, all while gracefully navigating the intricate complexities of ethical quandaries that frequently accompany such esteemed roles.

Leadership is a captivating and intricate concept, embodying a rich tapestry of abilities, characteristics, and conduct that ignite a collective vision and sway others to pursue common objectives and ambitions. At its core, leadership is rooted in a collection of essential principles that steer individuals in their pursuit of creating profound and enduring effects on their teams, enterprises, and societies.

In this endeavor, we will carefully analyze essential principles, including bravery, authenticity, faith, drive, and judgment, which are the foundation of effective leadership. These principles act as the cornerstone upon which outstanding leaders develop their aspirations, plans, and behaviors, leading them through both victories and challenges.

Nevertheless, the journey towards adept leadership is not devoid of obstacles and ethical intricacies. As leaders gracefully maneuver through the complexities of decision-making and moral dilemmas, they frequently encounter options that scrutinize their principles, uprightness, and commitment. These ethical predicaments represent pivotal moments for the cultivation of character, molding leaders into guardians of unwavering rectitude and moral resilience.

In the upcoming chapters, we will delve into practical examples and case studies that shed light on the intricacies of leadership and the ethical dilemmas that can arise in different organizational settings. Through the exploration of these challenges using fundamental leadership principles, our goal is to empower future leaders with the understanding, perspectives, and resources needed to effectively navigate the complexities of leadership with poise, honesty, and strength.

Core Concepts: Leadership

Courage: Courage is a fundamental pillar of effective leadership, embodying the readiness to embrace challenges, navigate risks, and endure difficult circumstances. Leaders of courage exemplify unwavering resolve and moral fortitude, making tough choices that others may avoid. They possess the audacity to advocate for their principles, even amidst dissent or disapproval. By demonstrating courageous leadership, they instill trust and cultivate a culture of perseverance among their teams, motivating individuals to explore new horizons, pioneer innovation, and strive for lofty aspirations.

Credibility: Cultivating credibility is an indispensable facet of exceptional leadership, for it engenders a profound sense of trust and admiration within one's team. Esteemed leaders embody unwavering honesty, integrity, and steadfastness in their every action and decision. They exemplify their core values and principles, serving as a beacon of inspiration and earning the unwavering trust of their followers. Transparent in their communication, credible leaders possess the humility to acknowledge missteps and assume accountability for their actions. Through unwavering reliability and unparalleled expertise, these remarkable leaders instill unwavering confidence and unwavering loyalty, thus fostering an environment that is both harmonious and highly productive.

Trust: Trust forms the bedrock upon which effective leadership and harmonious team dynamics are built. In order to gain the confidence and faith of their followers, leaders must exemplify unwavering integrity, exceptional competence, and unwavering reliability. Trustworthy leaders conduct themselves with utmost transparency in their communication, unwavering consistency in their actions, and unwavering accountability for their choices. They prioritize establishing and nurturing profound connections founded on mutual esteem and open dialogue. Trust, in turn, bestows upon team members the freedom to collaborate seamlessly, express their thoughts and ideas without reservation, and embrace calculated risks without trepidation of being unfairly judged or subjected to retribution. By fostering an environment of trust within a team, a remarkable sense of unity, loyalty, and unwavering dedication is cultivated, empowering the collective to confidently achieve its objectives.

Motivation: Motivation serves as the catalyst for successful leadership, spurring individuals to strive for greatness and unlock their true capabilities. Effective leaders inspire their teams by establishing definitive objectives, offering valuable feedback, and acknowledging accomplishments. They cultivate a nurturing and empowering atmosphere that fosters personal and professional development. Motivated leaders lead through their actions, showcasing enthusiasm, commitment, and fervor for their work. Their optimism, resilience, and adeptness at surmounting obstacles serve as a beacon of inspiration for others. By instilling a culture of motivation and positivity, leaders empower their teams to surmount challenges, seize opportunities, and achieve unparalleled levels of success.

Decision-Making: The art of effective decision-making is a crucial element of leadership, requiring a combination of astute judgment, strategic thinking, and the ability to assess risks and rewards. Leaders must be able to make difficult decisions while under pressure, taking into consideration the impact on their team, stakeholders, and the overall organization. They gather pertinent information, analyze data, and consult with key parties to make well-informed decisions. Successful leaders possess the ability to be decisive yet adaptable, willing to adjust their plans in response to changing circumstances. They take ownership of their choices, learn from setbacks, and constantly strive to enhance their decision-making abilities. Proficient decision-making empowers leaders to navigate complex obstacles, seize opportunities, and drive their teams toward triumph.

Moral Dilemmas

Moral dilemmas provide priceless teaching moments that promote both professional and personal development. People are forced to critically assess their values, beliefs, and principles in the face of ethical dilemmas, which helps them develop a better understanding of their unique moral core and ethical decision-making approach. People gain more self-awareness, empathy, and moral reasoning abilities when they wrestle with difficult decisions and weigh their ramifications. Moral conundrums also promote introspection, discussion, and cooperation, enabling people to gain knowledge from many viewpoints and methods of reaching moral decisions. You will develop resilience, integrity, and ethical leadership skills via these experiences, also enabling you to move wisely, compassionately, and honorably through challenging moral situations.

Loyalty Conflicts:

The intricate dilemma of loyalty conflicts frequently presents itself in leadership, as leaders find themselves torn between conflicting loyalties and responsibilities. These conflicts can take on diverse shapes, from conflicting allegiances to various team members, stakeholders, or organizational objectives. Successfully navigating loyalty conflicts demands that leaders delicately harmonize competing interests while remaining steadfast in their integrity and ethical values. Exemplary leaders approach loyalty conflicts with openness, truthfulness, and impartiality, ensuring that their decisions are driven by a dedication to the common good rather than personal prejudices or motives.

Transparency vs. Strategy:

Leaders face a delicate balance between being transparent and strategic in their communication with teams and stakeholders. While transparency builds trust and accountability, strategic discretion is necessary to protect sensitive information and maintain a competitive edge. Finding the right equilibrium between openness and strategy involves careful consideration of the risks and rewards of sharing information, all while ensuring that strategic goals remain intact. Successful leaders effectively navigate this balance by communicating openly when necessary and exercising discretion to safeguard organizational interests and promote a culture of trust and cooperation.

Taking Credit vs. Recognizing Team Efforts:

In the realm of leadership, one encounters a myriad of ethical quandaries, particularly when it pertains to the allocation of credit for triumphs, as opposed to acknowledging the invaluable contributions of team members. Although it may be alluring for leaders to claim exclusive recognition for accomplishments in order to bolster their standing or propel their own professional trajectory, such actions inevitably erode the morale, drive, and trust within their team. Conversely, by affording due recognition and celebrating the collective endeavors of team members, a culture of profound appreciation, collaboration, and reciprocal esteem is nurtured. Astute leaders prioritize virtues of modesty, integrity, and equity, ensuring that credit is justly distributed and that individual contributions are duly acknowledged and esteemed within the team.

Maintaining Equilibrium Between Short-Term Gains and Long-Term Impact:

Successful leaders must find a harmonious balance between pursuing immediate gains and prioritizing long-term sustainability and impact. While short-term gains may provide instant gratification, they can jeopardize future success and reputation. On the other hand, solely concentrating on long-term goals may overlook urgent issues that demand immediate action.

Effective leaders take a well-rounded approach, aligning short-term strategies with long-term goals, managing risks, and capitalizing on opportunities for sustainable growth. They emphasize strategic planning, flexibility, and responsiveness to ensure that their decisions lead to both short-term achievements and long-term value.

Making Tough Decisions in Limited Time:

In moments of urgency and complexity, leaders are faced with the demanding task of making difficult decisions within limited timeframes and high stakes. These decisions necessitate a careful balance of competing priorities, risks, and potential outcomes. Successful leaders approach these challenges with a clear mindset, unwavering focus, and composed demeanor, relying on their expertise, judgment, and moral compass to guide their choices. They diligently gather pertinent information, seek input from relevant parties, and carefully evaluate all potential consequences before taking decisive action. Despite the daunting nature of tough decisions, effective leaders view them as opportunities to demonstrate their courage, integrity, and resilience, even in the most challenging circumstances.

Chapter **14**

Speak as a Leader

Active public speaking enables leaders to refine their communication skills, confidence level, body language, and vocal delivery. Leaders who excel in public speaking can express their ideas compellingly and engagingly, resulting in communicating their thoughts in a better way. Whether you're addressing a small group of friends or speaking in front of a large audience, effective communication is key to influencing, inspiring, and leading others, giving them direction.

In this chapter, we will delve into the significance of active public speaking in leadership development, explore techniques for confident and persuasive speaking, provide you with bonus tips to overcome stage fright and nervousness and offer practice exercises for mastering your presentation and communication skills. Public speaking is not about conveying information. It's merely about how you connect with your audience and keep them engaged throughout your encouraging speech. For young adults, developing strong public speaking skills is particularly crucial as it lays the foundation for leadership roles in the future, which will make them great leaders. Active public speaking allows teenagers to articulate their ideas, gain confidence, and build credibility among their peers.

Public speaking allows you, as a leader, to show your team and your colleagues what you are thinking and what direction you want to take, and they will see you as not only an actual leader but also a thought leader. A leader isn't just someone who states what they want to be done and waits for people to do it. A leader is someone who motivates positive action, inspires innovation and growth, sets a set of goals for a group of people, and helps them find the path to their mutual success. There's no question that the only way that any of these ideals get accomplished is through clear communication — both as an active listener and speaker.

Why Teenagers Must Master Active Public Speaking?

Develops Communication Skills

Learning how to speak in public helps teenagers develop their communication skills. It is one of the most important ingredients for helping teenagers become leaders, as it helps youngsters convey their thoughts effectively. This encourages fluency and expands vocabulary among teenagers. Public speaking participates in the creation of communication skills among teenagers. The speaking abilities one possesses in front of others is a vital skill that can be game-changing in not only one's personal but also professional life. For teenagers, public speaking gives them not just the ability to impart their ideas and thoughts but also improve their communicative skills generally. As a result of constant rehearsals and being on a stage, teenagers get the experience of communicating their thoughts in a coherent manner, using proper language and intonation, and they are able to involve their audience effectively. In addition to that, teenagers, through public speaking, can learn to articulate and express their ideas very effectively. Language skills and knowledge of various vocabulary, fluency, and complex thinking are further improved through its use. They are crucial for effective leadership; leaders have to be able to set and spread a vision, achieve goals, and explain how to do that properly to everybody.

Builds Confidence

Public speaking can be intimidating, but learning how to speak in front of a large crowd confidently develops self-confidence. This will later help youngsters to voice their thoughts and opinions without any fear. Which allows them to voice their opinions, tell others what they think is right, and perform well even when there are difficulties. Leadership can be best achieved with the help of confidence, especially when leaders must act as the self-confident core to rally the confidence of their subordinates and peers. On top of it, the self-assurance that the teens might develop will contain inside them the courage to proceed beyond their comfort zones, be courageous, and try new activities that will determine their personal growth. Tackling the ability to speak in public has a positive side effect: the achieved self-relation immediately increases self-esteem and will influence the behavior of rarely giving up on following superior endeavors.

Enhances Critical Thinking

Writing speech typically requires your brain to think and analyze critically. Young people must research their topic, organize their thoughts, and decide how to present their information clearly and concisely with their gathered research. This will help teenagers to develop critical thinking skills to understand their topic. Public speaking strengthens the critical thinking capabilities of teenagers because they have to read and do research, organize their ideas, and then explain the information in a coherent and concise way. The steps that teenagers take before public speaking are collecting relevant information, evaluating sources, and data analysis to support their arguments. This way of learning trains analytical thinking and problem-solving skills, and teens will get more skilled in summarizing, identifying, and building arguments. Through questioning, analyzing, and reflecting on what they have learned about the problem, they improve their ability to problem-solve and develop a deeper understanding of complex issues. In addition, making information clear may necessitate teenagers to produce complex ideas briefly, which will make their critical thinking and communication skills even better.

Improves Leadership Qualities

Active public speaking helps teenagers to stand up for themselves and share their opinions about what they believe in and how to speak their minds without any hesitation or lack of confidence. They can inspire, motivate, and attract an audience with their words. One of the most important abilities of leaders is their capability to influence and motivate the people around them, which is a necessity for the completion of a lot of different tasks. Beyond this, being a part of an audience and delivering a speech is perfect for a young person's leadership skills and competence, such as making decisions, problem-solving, and communicating. When they take control of various leadership roles and speak of issues they are passionate about, adolescents showcase the capacity to have a firm sense of right and wrong and guide others through their strong examples, which earns them the admiration of their peers and mentors.

Active listener

Becoming a leader will make teenagers good listeners; they will listen to the queries and opinions of everyone like everyone else did when they were sharing their thoughts and opinions. In the age of the Internet, one of the most vital aspects of leadership is active listening, and teenagers are encouraged to be more attentive listeners through public speaking. While teenagers tend to be given opportunities to run for positions on boards and speeches at conventions, they become more aware of the need to pay attention to the questions and views of others with a sense of empathy and care. They actively listen to a variety of opinions and are able to evaluate others' perspectives, which, in turn, helps them create an environment of inclusion and cooperation where everybody's input is appreciated. This gives teenagers a sense of belonging and allows them to feel comfortable enough to speak openly, ultimately driving them to develop into successful team players. Also, being active listeners achieved through public speaking engagements upgrades teenagers in their ability to empathize with others, convey their message effectively, and solve their conflicts peacefully, thus developing their leadership.

Speaking Confidently

The key to confident speaking is thorough preparation. Research the topic thoroughly, including which you need to talk about and how you will deliver your message or speech, organize your thoughts, and outline your speech. Before going on a large platform, make sure to practice your speech multiple times, preferably in front of a mirror or with a friend. This will boost your confidence and help you refine your delivery and thoughts for later taking over on a larger platform.

When you speak, try to interact with your audience by asking questions, encouraging participation, or being realistic to gain most of your audience's attention and be relatable, which will open the barrier of trust and foster good communication. Maintain good posture throughout your speaking session, make eye contact with your audience, don't portray a defensive style, and use proper hand gestures to emphasize key points. Confident body language enhances your presence on stage. Cover voice modulation accordingly, such as varying your tone, pitch, and pace to keep your audience engaged.

A monotone delivery can dull the impact of your message, leaving the audience confused. Incorporating personal anecdotes or relevant stories to make your speech memorable and relatable will make more sense to your session as stories evoke emotions and capture the audience's attention. Positive thinking can make a huge difference in your speech, and it is the success of every communication skill. Don't make people think they cannot do specific tasks. Make them believe in themselves and hype them up for doing things that they desire to do. This will generate positive feedback towards your leadership journey.

Stage fright and nervousness are common among people; it is not something that only children can have. Most elderly people have this common fear. Teenagers think that they will go on stage, and suddenly, a tiger will appear and jump on them; people will start making fun of them or throw tomatoes at them, as they have seen in most cartoons and shows. But neither is true; it was all part of the script trying to make it look more interesting to the audience. If you want to overcome this fear and excel in leadership, then you can focus on some of the things to lift yourself from this fear:

> ➢ Practice deep breathing exercises to calm your nerves before speaking. Inhale deeply through your nose, hold for a few seconds, and exhale slowly through your mouth. Try to shift your mind from that particular session and just think you are casually

going towards your classroom and having a normal conversation with your classmates.

- ➤ Visualize yourself delivering a successful speech with confidence and poise. Imagine the audience reacting positively to your message; they will be happy and smiling throughout your speaking session. If you think someone is mocking you, you then divert your attention towards the audience that is happy to see you delivering the speech.

- ➤ Adopt a power pose, such as standing tall with your hands on your hips, to boost your confidence before taking the stage; show more hand gestures. This will shift your mind towards your hands, leaving you not thinking about your fear.

- ➤ Shift your focus from your nerves to the message you want to convey. Remember that your audience is interested in what you have to say, not in judging your performance. They only care about how well your message is conveyed and how powerful your message is.

- ➤ Practice mindfulness techniques, such as meditation or mindfulness exercises, to stay grounded and focused during your speech.

- ➤ Think you are just here to convey your message without worrying about becoming a people pleaser.

- ➤ Consider public speaking sessions, which will help you become a good speaker in the future. Watch podcasts that will motivate and encourage you to speak freely about your thoughts without worrying about what people will think.

Exercises for Effective Presentation Skills

I was in denial when I saw various dumb exercises on different websites teaching what you can do to excel in presentation skills. When I say dumb, I mean don't try these exercises. They will not help me become a better leader shortly. Before diving into this topic, let me clear one point: developing good leadership and presentation skills can take time. It's not something that you can master in one day. If you only drive a car once every two years, you will likely be terrified every time you get behind the wheel, so you should remain consistent with this and practice every day to help establish your presentation skills stronger.

Speak Up in Team Meetings: You have great ideas. Why not share them with your classmates? The biggest fear with public speaking is being judged by others, but don't worry about what others will think. Just present your point in front of others to let them know your opinion. When you see different people agreeing with your ideas and having different perspectives, you will get the value of your idea.

Peer Feedback: Seek feedback from friends or mentors on your speaking style, delivery, vocal delivery, body language, confidence level, and content, whether you were stuck to the topic throughout or your mind was diverted. Constructive criticism helps identify areas for improvement and how well you have tackled the presentation.

Design A Better Speech: All the exercises to improve your presentation skills will fail if you have created a terrible speech. Make your speech engaging by adding some humor and anecdotes in it to keep your audience engaged. Don't memorize your speech; just a thorough revision would be enough; otherwise, it will look like a robot is giving a presentation without modifying your voice.

Make A Speech On Personal Anecdote: If you want to be effective in your presentation skills, then you need to be a great storyteller. Try to tell your own story in your own words without modifying it; this will create trust between you and your audience, leaving you to master public speaking.

"Ninety percent of leadership is the ability to communicate something people want." - **Dianne Feinstein, U.S. Senator.**

Chapter **15**

Parent of a Leader

Parents play a pivotal role in shaping a teenager's life and helping them become better leaders. Parents can have a better influence on children after educational institutes. As parents, your influence extends beyond providing basic needs; you have the power to infuse values, cultivate confidence, and nurture leadership skills in your teenagers. In this chapter, we will explore the importance of parental support in fostering leadership development and discuss practical ways parents can actively contribute to their teenager's journey toward becoming a better leader. Love, support, trust, and optimism from family help children grow and become a better version of themselves; this will make them think of their worth and can achieve every milestone. Some parents struggle with the demands that they bring during their teenage years, but they should cater to their needs to help them become better leaders.

Emotional Support: Teenagers need a supportive and nurturing environment to thrive. Parents who provide emotional support create a safe space for their teenagers to explore their interests, take risks, and learn from failures. No matter how badly your children are performing, always maintain a positive attitude toward them; this will eliminate the factor of low self-confidence. This support bolsters their confidence and resilience, essential qualities for effective leadership.

Role Modeling: Parents serve as primary role models for their teenagers. By demonstrating strong leadership qualities such as integrity, empathy, and communication skills in their own lives, parents set a powerful example for their teenagers to emulate. Children often learn best by observing and imitating the behavior of their parents, trying to be more affectionate towards them, and giving a powerful example of a leader by listening to their problems and guiding them. Let your children express their own opinions and thoughts and give value to their thoughts.

Encouragement of Independence: Effective leaders are self-reliant and independent thinkers. Parents can encourage independence in their teenagers by empowering them to make decisions, solve problems, think on their own, and take responsibility for their actions. Offering guidance and encouragement while allowing teenagers to navigate challenges on their own fosters self-confidence and leadership skills.

Providing Opportunities for Growth: Parents can support their teenagers' leadership development by providing opportunities for growth and learning. This may include enrolling them in leadership programs, extracurricular activities, debate competitions, or volunteer opportunities where they can develop teamwork, communication, and problem-solving skills. Exposure to diverse experiences broadens their perspective and fosters leadership potential, this will help them in the future to tackle diverse problems in the future no matter how difficult the situation will be.

Open and Honest Communication: Effective communication is essential for building strong parent-teenager relationships. Parents who maintain open and honest communication channels with their teenagers create an environment where they feel valued, heard, and understood. Try not to disagree with their points and opinions harshly. Just politely disagree with them, giving a better opinion. This will not overshadow them in the future, and they will not feel disrespected. Encouraging dialogue allows parents to offer guidance, address concerns, and provide constructive feedback, promoting personal and leadership growth.

Parents' Role in Nurturing Leadership Skills in Children

Parents provide a safe and effective environment for their children. When children feel supported, they are more likely to express their thoughts not only to their parents but also to their classmates. Parents can help their teenagers discover their strengths, passions, and interests by actively engaging in conversations, observing their activities, and providing opportunities for exploration. Never force your children to make decisions and rules imposed by you it will shatter their power of decision-making. Ask your children about their area of interest and why they like that particular domain.

By identifying areas of talent and enthusiasm, parents can guide their teenagers toward activities and pursuits that align with their leadership potential. Parents should set high expectations for their teenagers, encourage them to strive for excellence in all endeavors, and never demean them if they do something that is not according to the parents' expectations. By believing in their teenagers' capabilities and holding them accountable for their actions, parents instill a sense of responsibility and ambition that is essential for leadership development.

Let your children solve their problems on their own without guiding them. Effective leaders are adept at finding solutions to challenges and overcoming obstacles, which will help them to overcome any hurdles in their lives. Parents can nurture their teenagers' problem-solving skills by encouraging critical thinking, creativity, and resilience. Encourage teenagers to approach problems analytically, brainstorm alternative solutions, and learn from setbacks. Create empathy and social awareness in your teenagers as they are fundamental qualities of effective leaders. Parents can cultivate these qualities in their teenagers by modeling empathy in their interactions, encouraging acts of kindness and compassion, creating a sense of generosity, excluding discrimination among races, and exposing them to diverse perspectives and experiences. Make them believe this; everyone has different opinions, and they should value everyone's opinion without disagreeing with it.

Encouraging teenagers to volunteer, participate in community service projects, or engage in discussions about social issues fosters empathy and social responsibility. Parents serve as mentors and guides in their teenagers' leadership journey. By offering guidance, encouragement, and constructive feedback, parents help their teenagers navigate challenges, set goals, and develop action plans for success. Creating a supportive and nurturing environment where teenagers feel empowered to pursue their dreams and aspirations is essential for their leadership development so that they can become successful leaders.

Encouraging Children to Adapt Leadership Skills

Every parent wants to see their children successful no matter in what domain they work. Parents naturally want their kids to be viewed as an inspiring and motivational leader. Developing leadership skills in your children requires lots of hard work and patience. Here is what you can do to see your child become a better leader:

- ➢ Teach your children to embrace failure without feeling inferior. Just like you accept the success of your children accept their failures as well this will have an appositive impact on your children. Becoming a leader means a teenager must be an optimistic person.
- ➢ Allow them to make their own decision, whether right or wrong. This will help them create solutions on their own rather than ask for help.
- ➢ Encourage them to play sports; as we all know, sports foster teamwork and help you understand the term "sportsmen spirit." This will allow your child to focus more on themselves and work hard.
- ➢ Patience is a skill that, when taught right can last a lifetime. Teach them to be patient with their decision and consider other people's decisions as well.

Case Study 1

Oprah Winfrey - Talk Show Host

Oprah Winfrey was born into poverty in rural Mississippi to a teenage mother. When she was six years old, her mother sent her to live with her maternal grandmother, Hattie Mae Lee, in Milwaukee, Wisconsin. Hattie Mae Lee, a strict disciplinarian, provided Oprah with a stable and structured environment that she lacked in her early childhood.

From a young age, Hattie Mae Lee instilled in Oprah the values of hard work, resilience, and determination. Despite their modest means, Hattie Mae Lee ensured that Oprah attended church regularly and focused on her education. She encouraged Oprah's love for reading and fostered her intellectual curiosity, laying the foundation for Oprah's future success.

Hattie Mae Lee's unwavering support and belief in Oprah's potential were instrumental in helping her overcome the trauma of her childhood abuse and poverty. She provided Oprah with a sense of security and self-worth, teaching her to be strong and independent.

Oprah has often spoken about how her grandmother's teachings and guidance helped her develop a strong work ethic and a resilient mindset. Hattie Mae Lee's emphasis on perseverance and determination inspired Oprah to pursue her dreams and never give up, even in the face of adversity.

When Oprah's career took off as a talk show host and media mogul, Hattie Mae Lee remained a constant source of support and grounding. Oprah has credited her grandmother for keeping her humble and reminding her of her roots, even as she achieved immense success.

Hattie Mae Lee's influence extended beyond Oprah's personal life; it also shaped her leadership style and philanthropic endeavors. Oprah's commitment to empowering others, particularly women and children, and her focus on education and personal growth can be traced back to the values instilled by her grandmother.

In many ways, Oprah Winfrey's remarkable journey from a childhood of poverty and abuse to becoming one of the most influential and successful leaders of our time is a testament to the transformative power of parental support and guidance, even in the face of overwhelming adversity.

Case Study 2

Barra - CEO of Major Automaker

From a young age, Ray Makela instilled in Mary Barra a strong work ethic and a sense of responsibility. As a die-maker at GM's Pontiac Motor Division, he would often bring Barra to the factory floor, exposing her to the world of manufacturing and the importance of hard work.

Makela taught Barra the value of problem-solving and taking ownership of her actions. He encouraged her to tackle challenges head-on, never make excuses, and take responsibility for her decisions. This mindset proved invaluable as Barra navigated her way through the ranks at GM, often in male-dominated environments.

Despite facing gender biases and societal expectations, Makela and Barra's mother, Eva, were unwavering in their support of their daughter's ambitions. They encouraged her to pursue her interests, including her love for mathematics, and never allowed gender to be a limitation.

Makela's emphasis on education and continuous learning also played a crucial role in Barra's development. He instilled in her a thirst for knowledge and a commitment to lifelong learning, qualities that have served her well in her leadership roles at GM.

As Barra progressed through various positions at GM, her father's lessons on perseverance and resilience became invaluable. Even when faced with setbacks or challenges, she remained determined and focused, drawing strength from the values instilled by her parents.

Makela's influence extended beyond just professional skills; he also taught Barra the importance of humility and staying grounded. Despite her achievements and success, Barra has remained approachable and connected to her roots, a trait she attributes to her father's guidance.

When Barra became the first female CEO of a major automaker in 2014, she acknowledged the pivotal role her parents played in her journey. She credited her father's lessons on hard work, problem-solving, and taking responsibility as the foundation for her leadership approach and her ability to navigate the challenges of leading a global company like GM.

Chapter **16**

Networking

Networking is a skill that only a few teenagers have learned and know about it. However, networking is a critical skill to know if you want to become a successful leader in the future. It can be beneficial in both social and professional aspects. Social networking can be defined as using different social media platforms to connect with others who have similar interests. This can also be your connections in the real world. Social networking also includes expressing your views, opinions, and thoughts to one another. Professional networking can be defined as building relationships with other professionals, either in your career or other related fields. Typically, this occurs at career fairs, conferences, and sometimes even social events. It's important to professionally network because of the opportunities that come with it.

Networking brings so many benefits that we may not think of. It also helps establish a connection between various people. A teenager who wants to be a successful leader in the future should know how to effectively use their network to establish strong relations with the use of their social networks to connect with fellow leaders and gain insights from them. They usually share their opinion and thoughts and create a link with all the successful leaders to become a good leader in the future.

Emerging trends will have leaders more and more using their networks to tackle complex issues and grasp opportunities in the fast-moving world arena. Having a network of peers, mentors, and industry professionals developed, honest teenagers can get nearly infinite wisdom and support to increase themselves as leaders and expand their careers. Additionally, networking acts as a source of support, connection, and togetherness that creates spaces for leaders to develop networks, aggregate resources, and propagate positive change in the corridors of their organizations and communities.

Also, networking allows leaders to keep up-to-date on developing trends, innovations, and best business practices, which translates into an edge in the competitive environment that is currently in the marketplace. Through meeting with and engaging thought leaders and influencers, teens will not only stay ahead of the trends but will also stand out and be seen as the new innovative and influential youth in their areas of interest.

Becoming Effective Leaders through Networking

In the digital world, social media platforms have been transformed into powerful facilities where teenagers have the opportunity to grow their leadership skills and the range of their networks. Teenagers have an array of possibilities at their disposal through social media, which includes connecting with their similar nature individuals, participating in online communities, and making their voices heard in a manner that puts them on a global scale.

The fact that social media is able to help networking and relationship building beyond geographical borders is yet another one of the numerous virtues that social media has got. These social platforms including LinkedIn, Twitter, and Instagram help teenagers to be connected to friends, mentors, and business people with diverse backgrounds, which currently forms a culture of collaboration among peers and knowledge sharing. Social media serves as a means to not only attract the interest of teenage audiences but also allows them to actively participate in discussions, share their particular ideas, and seek advice from experienced leaders who thus influence their worldview.

Social media is a very powerful tool that can shape the entire world within minutes. Firstly, social media provides teenagers with a platform to express their ideas, opinions, and perspectives with a global audience. Through blogging, or simply sharing posts, teenagers can articulate their thoughts on various issues, thus honing their articulation skills and communication skills which are vital for effective leadership. Moreover, the feedback and engagement received on social media help teenagers become more effective and think differently, bringing them a step closer to becoming successful leaders.

Secondly, social media allows teenagers to connect and collaborate with peers from different backgrounds and cultures making the teenagers think about different opinions and thoughts, what different people think according to their own cultures, and how they tackle the thoughts. Joining online communities, participating in groups, and taking part in different tasks will broaden the vision. These interactions help teenagers to learn from diverse groups, helping them reach their desired target of becoming good leaders.

Furthermore, a teenager can use social platforms to create their own identity by giving different opinions and thoughts to gather an audience, which will later help them. For instance, some teens make vlogs, some write blogs to express their views gauging people who have similar interests in any related topics. They can even write and publish books for more strong and permanent audiences so they will have more people in their support. Leadership quality includes being updated with any current events and emerging trends so, teenagers can gather information on any topic which they want to express their views with reliable and authentic information so they can have a valid point to present in front of their followers as social media is a very powerful tool.

Social media plays a powerful role in helping teenagers to become powerful leaders. Social media presents a way of showing up for teen leaders so that they can put up their talents, achievements, and ideas in front of more people. Through the creation of a distinctive brand and by disseminating quality information, teenagers can position themselves as serious professionals in their niches who people tend to listen to. Social media breaks the communication barrier by allowing for multi-media formats, which include videos, infographics, and podcasts, for young adults to effectively deliver their messages and engage the community.

Building Networks as a New Leader

When you're trying to make connections with people for your career, it's important to focus on meeting the right people who can help you in a good way instead of trying to meet as many people as possible. Instead of just going to events and giving out your contact information, try to build relationships with people who can really make a difference in your job or career. Remembering their names is an important part of building a strong network of people to help you.

It's important to make sure that everyone involved in a networking relationship benefits in order to create a positive and long-lasting connection. When both people gain something from the relationship, it helps build trust and makes the partnership stronger.

When you talk to people and make connections, it's good to both ask for help and offer help. By helping others, you show that you are friendly and kind. This can make the relationship stronger and encourage others to help you, too. It's like being a good friend and helping each other out.

Being a connector means helping people in your group connect with others who can help them or work with them. It's like being a bridge between different people, which can make your relationships stronger and create more chances for good things to happen. If you're known as a connector, it can make your networking even better and help you find new and great partnerships.

When you meet new people and want to be friends with them, it's important to keep talking to them and checking in with them regularly. This helps you build a strong friendship and show that you care about them. Sending them messages or asking how they are doing every once in a while can help you stay close and remind them how important they are to you.

Using websites like LinkedIn, Facebook, and Twitter can help you make new friends and learn new things about the job you want. You can meet people who work in the same field as you and find out about job opportunities. On LinkedIn, you can even meet new people through friends you already know.

Creating your own networking group means gathering people who have similar interests or work in the same industry. By planning events and activities around specific topics, you can meet new friends and people who share your goals. Being a leader in the group can help you make new connections and become an important person in your professional community.

Effective Leadership Networking

Now that you've taken the steps to build leadership networks, you have to maintain their effectiveness and robustness, too. To achieve this, the following 6 factors will be vital components:

1. **Sincerity:** The primary key to maintaining a network is sincerity. As a leader who built his own network, you should be sincere and honest towards everyone. People's views about you matter, especially when you are the leader. If you have a bad reputation, your network won't take long enough to shut down permanently. Let's be honest, everyone loves a sincere leader who works hard to facilitate everyone, gives respect and earns it back by their actions.

2. **Sharing Resources:** Sometimes people within the network need some additional help either via means of knowledge, services, or resources. As a leader, you should learn the skill of sharing resources among the networks in a way, that the truly needy ones avail them. This encourages the network members to exchange valuable resources with each other.

3. **Using Power Appropriately:** A leader must understand the importance of power in effective leadership networking. If you misuse your power, karma will

get back to you, and at that time, you will regret it. You should aim to be the leader who ensures the power is used appropriately to assist the ones who need help and take care of those who are rude and aggressive. An effective network needs a true yet compassionate leader.

4. **Effective and Skilled Communication:** As a leader trying to maintain their network, effective communication is significant in sharing their goals with the network. Making yourself understood will help you convey your needs and what you can offer to them. If you are good at communicating, your networking strategies won't be in vain.

5. **Negotiation:** Being good at negotiating is really important for leaders because it helps them keep their friends and work well with other people. When leaders know how to negotiate, they can figure out how to make everyone happy and get what they want. Good negotiators know how to be firm about some things but also know when to give in and make compromises. Being good at negotiating helps leaders make friends in their network and be trusted, which helps them reach their goals.

6. **Conflict Management:** It's important for leaders to know how to deal with disagreements in the group of people they lead. Conflicts happen sometimes, and how leaders handle them can make a big difference in their relationships and influence. By learning how to solve conflicts peacefully, leaders can keep their group strong and work well together. Listening to others, trying to understand their side, and finding ways to agree are all ways leaders can make their network better.

Chapter **17**

Is Inclusive Leadership a Thing?

Inclusive leadership represents a profound and influential style of leadership that embraces the concepts of diversity, equity, and belonging within various settings, including organizations and communities. At its essence, inclusive leadership endeavors to establish environments that cultivate a sense of worth, admiration, and empowerment for each individual, enabling them to contribute their distinctive insights and abilities. These exceptional leaders acknowledge the intrinsic value of diversity and diligently work towards nurturing inclusive cultures that not only appreciate disparities but also advocate for fairness and equity. By embracing inclusivity, leaders effectively tap into the collective strengths of diverse teams, thereby fostering innovation, creativity, and overall organizational effectiveness.

Dedication lies at the core of inclusive leadership, exemplifying a leader's unyielding devotion to fostering diversity, equity, and inclusion within their organization. Committed leaders place utmost importance on inclusivity when making decisions, establishing policies, and implementing practices, showcasing their genuine dedication to creating opportunities for every individual to flourish and prosper. They wholeheartedly champion initiatives that embrace diversity, allocate resources towards fostering inclusion, and uphold themselves and others responsible for advancing equity and impartiality. Through their unwavering commitment, inclusive leaders inspire confidence, involvement, and a profound sense of belonging among team members, propelling positive transformations within the organization.

The ability to navigate diverse cultural contexts with sensitivity, respect, and understanding is crucial for effective inclusive leadership. Culturally intelligent leaders possess the awareness, knowledge, and skills to bridge cultural differences, build meaningful relationships, and create inclusive environments where everyone feels valued and respected. By actively seeking to understand and appreciate diverse perspectives and traditions, these leaders can leverage cultural differences as strengths rather than barriers. Cultivating cultural intelligence fosters a culture of inclusivity, collaboration, and innovation that transcends cultural boundaries and promotes mutual respect and understanding.

Collaboration is a fundamental aspect of inclusive leadership, highlighting the significance of working together harmoniously, communicating effectively, and cooperating across various viewpoints and experiences. Inclusive leaders cultivate a space where all perspectives are acknowledged, appreciated, and honored, promoting open discussions, idea generation, and collaborative problem-solving. They facilitate collaboration by dismantling barriers, nurturing relationships across different departments, and providing platforms for diverse teams to collaborate and innovate together. By fostering effective collaboration, inclusive leaders leverage the diverse talents and innovative ideas of their teams, ultimately driving creativity, adaptability, and overall success within the organization.

Inclusive leaders embrace humility as a cornerstone of their leadership style, recognizing the importance of acknowledging their own shortcomings and valuing the perspectives of others. They create a welcoming and authentic environment where team members feel empowered to share their thoughts and concerns. By actively seeking out diverse viewpoints and demonstrating empathy and compassion, humble leaders foster a culture of trust and continuous learning, ensuring that everyone feels valued and supported in contributing their best.

The concept of fair treatment lies at the core of inclusive leadership, highlighting the values of equality, fairness, and dignity towards all individuals, irrespective of their backgrounds. Inclusive leaders aim to establish a fair and just environment where everyone is given equal opportunities, resources, and acknowledgment based on their abilities and efforts. They champion fairness and equity in all aspects of organizational practices, policies, and decision-making processes, confronting bias, prejudice, and unfairness whenever they surface. Through advocating for fair treatment, inclusive leaders foster a culture of trust, responsibility, and inclusion, enabling individuals to excel and fulfill their potential, regardless of their diversity.

Cultural Competency: Definition and its Role in Leadership

Similarly, the concept of cultural competence plays a significant role in the character development of a leader. For those, who aren't familiar with the term cultural competence, it is the skill of a leader to engage and communicate effectively with individuals from various cultural backgrounds while showing respect, empathy, and understanding towards their perspectives and experiences. In the universe of character development, cultural competency plays a crucial role in fostering inclusive leadership qualities like empathy, open-mindedness, and versatility. Culturally competent leaders acknowledge the importance of diversity and make an effort to comprehend and value the distinct cultural backgrounds, beliefs, and experiences of their team members. By honing their cultural competency, leaders can strengthen their capacity to form meaningful connections, promote inclusivity, and navigate intricate cultural dynamics in their organizations and communities.

If we take a look at the essence of an authentic leader, it is a person who is true and loyal to what they firmly believe in. Such leaders realize what the actual meaning of leadership is and its purpose. Most of them steer their lives with the consistent values of leadership residing in their hearts. But, if we question what it means to be a true and genuine leader, we come across the following;

- ➢ Lead with the accurate values of leadership; moreover, leading with heart and mind together makes them more passionate and attentive.
- ➢ Authentic leaders are result-oriented; they work hard and guide their teams accordingly to ensure the targeted missions are achieved in a timely manner.
- ➢ Mark their eyes on long-term results rather than shortcuts and short-term goals.
- ➢ Are culturally competent to help other team members regardless of their background, race, etc.

There is another mention of cultural competency in leadership: how can you obtain this skill? Before that, we must understand the relationship between cultural competency and true leadership. The foundation of a culturally competent leader is someone who understands his team members better, which will result in a better form of communication and interaction. Effective communication between teams will help deliver exceptional results without any hassle. It's not a characteristic that most people have from the beginning; rather, it takes time to develop.

In easier words, being true to yourself and understanding different cultures go hand in hand. It's important to be aware of your own biases and be open to learning and changing. Do you understand why adaptability is also a vital characteristic of leaders?

Being true in team relationships means being honest about who you are and also being kind to other people's feelings and beliefs. It's important to know and understand your own values and to be aware of how you might see things differently from others. Cultural competence means being able to get along and talk with people from different cultures. It's about understanding and respecting that people have different ways of doing things and different beliefs.

Knowing and understanding yourself is really important when interacting with people from different cultures. By recognizing your own beliefs and how they affect how you see things, you can better understand how they might impact your relationships and choices. Brackets are like special tools that help us understand and appreciate different cultures. When we use brackets, it means we put aside any ideas or opinions we have about other cultures. This helps us to be open-minded and not judge others based on what we think we know. By doing this, we can better understand and care about how other people see the world.

It's important for leaders to understand how their personal opinions can affect how they lead. They need to realize that their opinions can change how they see things, make choices, and treat people, especially those from different cultures. When leaders acknowledge these opinions, they can try to lessen their impact and make sure everyone feels important and treated well.

Being willing to recognize and work on our biases is really important for being true to ourselves and understanding different cultures. It means we need to think about our biases, learn about them, and keep learning. When we do this, we can build real connections with others and learn more about different ways of thinking. Overall, being true to yourself and understanding and respecting different cultures are important. When we are authentic and open-minded, we can connect with others and make everyone feel included, hence developing a collaborative work environment.

Developing Cultural Competence

A leader should work on becoming culturally competent. It is equally important to know how to set an unforgettable tone for your team and positively interact with people from distinct backgrounds. If you want to thrive as a true leader in this century, you must have the capability to dive into the world of diverse cultures and be culturally intelligent, which is a blend of cultural competency and emotional intelligence. Cultural intelligence, as seen through the eyes of a leader, is the capacity to recognize, adapt, and respect cultural differences in order to effectively lead diverse teams. It entails being aware of the customs, attitudes, and expectations of various cultural contexts and modifying one's leadership style accordingly.

1. **Valuing and Promoting Continuous Learning:** Rather than developing an attitude and ego, culturally competent leaders are learning continuously from their teams. We can all agree that irrespective of how much knowledge you possess, skills you learned, or awareness you have, there will always be a minor or major room for growth. You can begin your very own journey of continuous learning by

trying new things, asking for help from your team members, reflecting on the mistakes you made, accepting you have limited knowledge and skills, acknowledging the room for growth, and getting enrolled in some training programs.

2. **Making Bold Decisions:** Mistakes, from a unique perspective, are the perfect opportunities for learning, and that's why leaders aren't afraid of making mistakes. Even though they are stuck in their responsibilities and core values, they have the tendency to try new things. This means making bold choices, and that includes taking risks irrespective of the outcomes to find different solutions to many problems, overcoming the discomfort when learning and trying new things, and sticking by the core values without violating anyone.

3. **Researching and Collaborating with Teams:** Not all decisions are made boldly; culturally competent leaders consider everyone's perspectives before finalizing a decision. They ensure the decision doesn't affect any other person negatively. To research and collaborate, one has to get an overview of all the data to back up one's decision. A true leader will ask for advice from senior members and their responses. Moreover, the leader will work with other departments to address the concurrent issues.

4. **Developing well-thought-out and strategic plans:** It's important to make good plans that think about different cultures so that everyone can understand and work well with people from diverse backgrounds. By doing research and thinking carefully, a leader can learn about how different people do things and talk to each other. Then, use the information to make plans that are fair and include everyone. Planning also helps us figure out problems that might come up because of cultural differences and make a plan to solve them. This helps a leader become better at understanding and working with different cultures, hence developing cultural competency.

5. **Open to communication:** Being open to talking and listening to your team, which comprises people from different cultures, is really important. It helps them learn from each other and understand each other better. When we listen to others and try to understand their experiences and beliefs, we become better at getting along with people from different cultures. It also helps us work together and be friends with people from different backgrounds.

Bust The Bias

Addressing bias and breaking down stereotypes are important aspects of effective leadership because they promote inclusivity, equity, and equity within organizations and communities. Leaders play a vital role in challenging stereotypes and bias by fostering awareness, dialogue, and action to promote diversity and inclusion. Here are some strategies for leaders to address bias and bust through stereotypes:

Promote Education and Awareness: Leaders have the remarkable ability to cultivate an atmosphere of enlightenment and persuasion within their organizations, wherein the values of education and awareness concerning unconscious bias and stereotypes are upheld. This can be achieved through the provision of meticulously designed training sessions, enriching workshops, and invaluable resources, all aimed at equipping team members with the discernment and courage to identify and confront their biases. By promoting a culture that thrives on perpetual learning, leaders empower individuals to transcend their limitations and embrace a state of heightened consciousness and inclusivity in their every interaction and decision-making process.

Lead by Example: Leaders play a crucial role in fostering an inclusive environment by exemplifying inclusive behaviors through their actions and words. By actively embracing diversity, challenging preconceived notions, and advocating for fairness, leaders serve as role models and encourage others to cultivate a culture of inclusivity and respect.

Encourage Dialogue and Collaboration: Leaders have the ability to cultivate an environment of open discourse and collective effort within their teams, aimed at effectively addressing prejudice and preconceived notions in a manner that is both constructive and dignified. Through the establishment of secure platforms for dialogue and the encouragement of personal storytelling, leaders facilitate profound and impactful conversations that actively question presumptions, expand horizons, and foster a culture of comprehension and compassion.

Empower Diverse Voices: Leaders should proactively and magnify a multitude of voices within their organizations, guaranteeing that every team member is given the chance to contribute their distinctive viewpoints and ideas. Through the establishment of platforms for marginalized individuals to articulate their experiences and wisdom, leaders cultivate a culture characterized by inclusivity and a sense of belonging, where each individual is esteemed and honored.

Implement Bias-Mitigating Strategies: Leaders have the power to seamlessly incorporate effective strategies into their hiring, promotion, and decision-making processes, thereby gracefully diminishing the effects of unconscious bias and championing principles of justice and equality. This can be achieved through the utilization of refined interview techniques, the establishment of diverse hiring panels, and the seamless implementation of blind resume reviews, all aimed at mitigating bias and guaranteeing that decisions are made solely on the basis of merit and qualifications.

Through the implementation of these tactics and the deliberate effort to confront prejudice and preconceived notions, leaders have the opportunity to cultivate environments that are not only inclusive and fair but also where individuals feel appreciated, esteemed, and confident in their ability to thrive. By taking a stand against bias and promoting a culture of acceptance, diversity, and unity, leaders serve as catalysts for positive change within their communities and organizations.

Chapter **18**

Reflective Leadership

Self-reflection is a crucial component of a leader's development, especially in today's fast-paced and unpredictable world. In order to thrive in this ever-changing environment, leaders must continuously evolve, think creatively, and motivate their teams to overcome obstacles and embrace new possibilities. Through self-reflection, leaders can improve their leadership skills, stimulate personal growth, and gain a deeper insight into their own actions and influence on those around them.

Above all, the practice of self-reflection empowers leaders to attain a profound understanding of their values, convictions, and aspirations. Through the ongoing scrutiny of their thoughts, sentiments, and conduct, leaders are able to discern their fundamental principles and evaluate the congruence between their actions and their ideals. This heightened self-awareness serves as the bedrock of genuine leadership, enabling leaders to guide with unwavering integrity and foster unwavering trust amongst their teams. In a world that increasingly cherishes transparency and ethical behavior, leaders who embrace the art of self-reflection emerge as adept navigators of principled decision-making, steadfastly upholding their moral compass.

Engaging in self-reflection allows leaders to assess their own strengths and weaknesses impartially. This introspective process enables leaders to identify areas in need of improvement and actively pursue opportunities for personal and professional growth. By leveraging their strengths and addressing any limitations, leaders can effectively drive success. Embracing a growth mindset, leaders can continuously develop new skills, expand their viewpoints, and navigate changing situations with adaptability and resilience.

Self-reflection cultivates empathy and emotional intelligence in leaders, crucial attributes for establishing genuine connections and promoting teamwork within diverse groups. Through introspection of their own emotions and experiences, leaders can gain a deeper insight into the thoughts and feelings of others. This heightened sense of empathy equips leaders to communicate more efficiently, address conflicts positively, and nurture the welfare of their team members. In a time marked by swift technological progress and digital interactions, leaders who prioritize human connection through self-reflection have the ability to establish inclusive and encouraging work atmospheres where individuals can flourish and bring their utmost contributions.

Your regular practice of self-reflection empowers you to derive meaningful insights from your past experiences and adjust your leadership approach accordingly. By analyzing both their triumphs and setbacks, leaders can extract valuable lessons that inform their future decisions and behaviors. This ongoing cycle of reflection and adjustment enables leaders to continuously enhance their leadership style, explore innovative tactics, and anticipate and address emerging obstacles. In a rapidly changing business environment, leaders who prioritize self-reflection and continual learning are better positioned to navigate uncertainty and facilitate long-term success.

Self-Reflection Tools

Self-reflection and the act of documenting one's thoughts and experiences offer tremendous value to those who aspire to evolve personally, advance professionally, and cultivate a heightened sense of self-awareness. These exceptional resources, known as self-assessment and journaling tools, offer meticulously designed structures and thought-provoking prompts that effortlessly guide individuals toward introspection, contemplation, and the establishment of meaningful objectives. By immersing themselves in the practice of self-assessment and journaling, individuals unlock profound insights into their innermost musings, emotions, strengths, and areas in need of refinement. This transformative process ultimately empowers individuals to make well-informed choices and embrace lives brimming with fulfillment and purpose.

Self-assessment tools encompass a range of sophisticated questionnaires, surveys, and assessments meticulously crafted to assess the multifaceted dimensions of an individual's personality, skills, values, and behaviors. Rooted in the depths of psychological theories, these tools delve into the profound realms of personality traits and emotional intelligence, yielding a comprehensive understanding of one's unique disposition and proclivities. By embarking on this introspective journey, individuals are empowered to unearth their inherent strengths, confront their vulnerabilities, and identify untapped areas of personal growth. Armed with such profound insights, they are poised to make judicious choices regarding their career trajectories, interpersonal connections, and aspirations for self-improvement.

Myers-Briggs Type Indicator (MBTI) is a widely acclaimed self-assessment tool that classifies individuals into distinct personality types, guided by their inclinations in four significant domains: extraversion versus introversion, sensing versus intuition, thinking versus feeling, and judging versus perceiving. By comprehending their MBTI type, individuals can obtain valuable insights into their unique communication style, decision-making methodology, and interpersonal dynamics, ultimately enhancing their leadership capabilities and fostering harmonious teamwork.

The StrengthsFinder assessment is a highly regarded self-assessment tool that unveils an individual's top strengths from a comprehensive list of 34 talent themes. By acknowledging and harnessing these inherent abilities, individuals can elevate their performance in the workplace, foster cohesive team dynamics, and attain their objectives with enhanced assurance and fulfillment.

Furthermore, alongside the utilization of self-assessment tools, the art of journaling presents a profound avenue for profound self-reflection and introspection. Engaging in the practice of journaling entails the consistent act of transcribing one's thoughts, emotions, encounters, and perceptions within the confines of a personal diary or digital medium. Through the act of committing their musings to paper, individuals can attain a heightened sense of lucidity, navigate intricate sentiments, and meticulously monitor their personal growth throughout the passage of time.

The art of journaling encompasses a wide range of techniques, such as the liberating act of free-writing, guided prompts that offer structure, the transformative practice of gratitude journaling, or the empowering process of goal-setting exercises. Whether one chooses to engage in daily introspection or opts for more periodic reflections, journaling offers a sanctuary where individuals can delve into their deepest emotions and musings, free from the shackles of judgment or critique.

Additionally, journaling can be utilized as a sophisticated instrument for establishing and monitoring both personal and professional aspirations. Through the act of meticulously documenting goals, delineating them into manageable tasks, and contemplating progress made, individuals can maintain a sense of direction, drive, and self-responsibility. Moreover, journaling offers a platform for acknowledging accomplishments, gleaning valuable lessons from setbacks, and adapting goals accordingly, thereby cultivating a mindset of continuous growth and unwavering resilience when confronted with obstacles.

To encapsulate, the utilization of self-assessment and journaling tools presents an exquisite opportunity for individuals yearning for self-discovery, personal advancement, and career elevation. Whether engaging in meticulously designed evaluations or indulging in introspective journaling rituals, individuals can luxuriate in profound revelations regarding their aptitudes, vulnerabilities, principles, and aspirations. This empowerment enables them to diligently forge deliberate paths and embrace lives replete with profound fulfillment. By seamlessly integrating the practices of self-assessment and journaling into their daily routines, individuals unlock unparalleled clarity, purpose, and authenticity that cascade effortlessly into both their personal and professional spheres.

Example 1:

Elon Musk – CEO Tesla & SpaceX

Elon Musk, the visionary driving force behind groundbreaking companies such as Tesla and SpaceX, embodies true leadership by envisioning a future that is nothing short of extraordinary. Musk's relentless determination to revolutionize transportation and propel humanity into a multi-planetary era has mesmerized the global community. His innate capacity to motivate and ignite his teams to embrace audacious aspirations and redefine the limits of innovation has fundamentally transformed industries, igniting a profound surge of technological progress.

Example 2:

Rosa Parks – Mother of Civil Rights

Parks is renowned as the inspirational figurehead of the Civil Rights Movement in America. Through her courageous refusal to surrender her seat on a segregated bus, she catalyzed a transformative moment in the struggle for racial justice. Parks' bold defiance and her significant contributions to the civil rights cause serve as a poignant reminder of the transformative impact that individual bravery can have on society as a whole.

Example 3:

Winston Churchill – The Real Leader

Winston Churchill, the esteemed Prime Minister of the United Kingdom throughout the tumultuous period of World War II, exemplified unparalleled leadership as he united his nation and instilled a sense of unwavering fortitude in the face of immense challenges. His resolute decision-making and inspirational rhetoric stand as a shining example of the transformative impact a steadfast leader can have in times of crisis.

Case Study: Failure

Jeffery S. Russell – Professor at the University of Wisconsin

Sometimes, things don't go as planned, and we experience failures. It's important to learn from these failures and use them to become better leaders. Reflecting on what went wrong helps us make better decisions in the future. Failure doesn't just mean making a mistake; it can also mean missing out on an opportunity. I learned this lesson when I got injured during a football game and had to give up my dreams of playing in college. I had to come up with a new plan and focus on my education instead. I struggled with writing, but I practiced and got better with the help of my teachers. I learned that when we face challenges, we need to work hard to improve ourselves. It's also important to seek support from our community when we're struggling.

Later on, I went to another school to study more and get a higher degree. But during an important test, I got asked a lot of hard questions that I didn't know the answers to. It made me want to give up, but my advisor told me that the test was meant to show me that I still had a lot to learn. I learned that it's important to always be prepared and keep learning because there's always more to know.

When I became the head of a department at the university, I made a lot of changes right away. But some people didn't like it, and I learned that it's important to be patient when leading others. Sometimes, you have to wait and listen to what others want. I was stuck in a tough situation and couldn't get out by myself. Luckily, some really nice people from the engineering department helped me and encouraged me. They told me that it's okay to struggle sometimes and that other students have gone through similar things. The teachers also helped me make a plan to get back on track. My family and friends were there for me, too, and it made me realize how important it is to have people who support you.

I wanted to be a professor at a university, but it wasn't easy to get there. I got rejected by a few schools before finally getting a job at the University of Wisconsin-Madison. Even though I didn't get what I wanted right away, I learned a lot about myself and how to communicate with others. The process of trying and failing was valuable in itself. Lastly, I had an important role in a committee that was trying to change some rules for civil engineers. We made progress but couldn't get it approved. Eventually, they asked me to leave the committee. It was disappointing, but it taught me that sometimes you have to know when to move on. I should have left earlier and had a plan for what to do next.

The lesson is that it's okay to ask for help and have people support you. You have to keep learning and be prepared for challenges. Sometimes, you'll hear "no" a lot before you hear "yes." And it's important to be patient and know when it's time to move on to something new.

Chapter **19**

Technology is Your Friend

In today's modern world, the fusion of leadership and technology is undeniable, as technology continues to significantly impact the way leadership is executed and organizational structures operate. This intricate relationship between leadership and technology encompasses various elements such as communication, creativity, strategic decision-making, and the overall ethos of an organization.

The convergence of leadership and technology is most prominently demonstrated through the avenue of communication. Innovations in technology, including email, instant messaging, video conferencing, and social media platforms, have transformed the manner in which leaders engage with their teams, stakeholders, and wider communities. Through these advancements, leaders are able to engage with individuals across distances instantaneously, promoting collaboration, knowledge dissemination, and the cultivation of relationships. Skillful leaders utilize technology to cultivate transparency, accessibility, and inclusivity in their communication strategies, guaranteeing that their messages are effectively conveyed to diverse audiences through suitable mediums.

Technology acts as a powerful force for driving innovation and transformation within organizations, and effective leadership is vital in spearheading technological advancements. Leaders play a pivotal role in presenting a compelling vision for how technology can be utilized to achieve strategic goals, enhance operational efficiency, and elevate customer experiences. By cultivating a culture of experimentation, taking calculated risks, and promoting continuous learning, leaders have the ability to ignite creativity and foster innovation across the organization. Additionally, strong leadership is essential in navigating the complexities and obstacles posed by technological disruptions, including cybersecurity risks, data privacy issues, and workforce automation, to ensure that organizations not only adapt but thrive in a swiftly evolving digital environment.

Leaders obtain an invaluable opportunity to access extensive pools of data and analytics, serving as a catalyst for informed decision-making and the enhancement of performance. By harnessing the power of data-driven insights, leaders can attain a profound comprehension of prevailing market trends, customer inclinations, and key performance indicators within their organizations. This, in turn, empowers them to make judicious strategic choices while efficiently allocating resources. Through the utilization of cutting-edge technologies such as artificial intelligence, machine learning, and predictive analytics, leaders are able to discern patterns, forecast future trends, and optimize business operations, ultimately securing a competitive edge within the ever-evolving marketplace.

It is important to recognize the profound impact of technology on the culture within organizations and the level of engagement among employees. Effective leadership is absolutely crucial to successfully navigate the intricacies of digital transformation and cultivate an environment characterized by agility, adaptability, and innovation. Therefore, leaders must prioritize the establishment of a supportive and inclusive workplace where individuals feel empowered to embrace technology, explore novel tools and approaches, and embrace changing roles and responsibilities. By championing a culture that emphasizes continuous learning, collaboration, and transparent communication, leaders have the ability to fully harness the extraordinary potential of technology in order to enhance employee engagement, bolster productivity, and ultimately foster a sense of fulfillment and satisfaction in the workplace.

Making Technology Your Friend

The art of effective leadership in utilizing technology involves a comprehensive approach that combines technical expertise, strategic foresight, and exceptional interpersonal abilities. Primarily, leaders must possess an in-depth understanding of the ever-evolving technological landscape within their respective industries, enabling them to identify advantageous prospects for leveraging technology to achieve strategic objectives and propel organizational growth. Furthermore, exceptional leaders cultivate an environment of innovation and experimentation, encouraging their teams to embrace emerging technologies, adapt to digital transformations, and explore novel approaches to their work. By providing the necessary resources, training, and support, leaders empower their teams to fully harness the potential of technology, optimizing productivity, streamlining processes, and delivering exceptional value to customers. Moreover, strong leadership is imperative when it comes to navigating the ethical, legal, and social implications of technology, ensuring that organizations prioritize responsible and sustainable usage while effectively managing risks and addressing concerns.

In today's digital age, it is imperative for young leaders to possess proficient digital communication skills. These encompass the ability to effectively convey ideas, collaborate with others, and build relationships using digital platforms and tools. Firstly, teenagers must excel in written communication, including etiquette in emails, messaging apps, and social media, to express their thoughts clearly and professionally. Moreover, they should develop strong verbal communication skills for virtual meetings, presentations, and video conferences, ensuring their ability to confidently articulate ideas and engage with peers and stakeholders. Additionally, active listening skills are crucial, enabling teenagers to understand others' perspectives, empathize with their experiences, and forge meaningful connections in digital environments. Furthermore, they should demonstrate digital literacy, encompassing critical thinking, information literacy, and media literacy, to navigate the intricacies of online communication, identify credible sources, and assess the validity and reliability of digital content. By honing these digital communication skills, teenagers can establish themselves as effective leaders in the digital era, inspiring others, fostering collaboration, and making a positive impact in their communities and organizations.

Collaboration Tools

There is an abundance of collaboration tools available online that cater to team leadership, presenting a wide array of features and functionalities aimed at facilitating communication, coordination, and project management. One particularly well-regarded collaboration tool is **Slack**, which offers real-time messaging, file sharing, and seamless integration with other productivity tools, enabling teams to communicate and collaborate effortlessly across various channels and projects. Additionally, **Microsoft Teams** provides an all-encompassing suite of communication and collaboration features, including video conferencing, document collaboration, and task management, all seamlessly integrated with the **Microsoft Office 365 ecosystem**.

Furthermore, project management tools like **Trello**, **Asana**, and **Monday.com** present intuitive interfaces that simplify the organization of tasks, establishment of priorities, and tracking of progress, empowering teams to work efficiently and effectively towards their shared goals. Moreover, collaboration tools such as **Google Workspace (formerly G Suite)** offer a suite of productivity applications, including **Gmail**, **Google Drive**, and **Google Meet**, allowing teams to collaborate on documents, spreadsheets, and presentations in real time. By harnessing the power of these collaboration tools, team leaders can strengthen communication, streamline workflows, and cultivate collaboration among team members, ultimately driving productivity and successfully attaining shared objectives in virtual and distributed work environments.

Chapter **20**

Final Verdict

As we near the end of our exploration in " Growing Leaders: Empowering Leadership and Management Skills in Your Teenage Child," it is crucial to contemplate the vast reservoir of wisdom and perspectives acquired along the way. This book has served as a thorough manual for fostering leadership qualities in young individuals, providing them with the resources, understanding, and mindset required to excel in the fast-paced environment of the present day.

In our journey through the chapters, we have delved deep into the very core of leadership, thoroughly examined a multitude of leadership styles, refined our communication abilities, analyzed the intricate art of decision-making, and successfully maneuvered through the challenges of conflicts and teamwork dynamics. Moreover, we have meticulously explored the significance of effective time management, personal introspection, emotional intelligence, ethical conduct, persuasive public speaking, invaluable parental guidance, building a strong network, and embracing inclusive leadership. Each of these subjects has been carefully crafted to deliver not only actionable strategies and practical advice but also real-life case studies that will ignite inspiration and empower the young leaders of tomorrow.

In the concluding section, we emphasize the harmonious connection between leadership and technology, underscoring the crucial role of strong leadership in maximizing the potential of technological advancements. We have delved into the significance of digital communication proficiency for young leaders and showcased the various online collaboration tools that can aid in effective team leadership. By embracing and integrating technology into their leadership approach, teenagers can elevate their leadership skills, foster meaningful connections, and inspire positive transformation in both their local communities and the world at large.

As we come to the end of this journey, let us not forget that true leadership transcends mere titles and positions. It is rooted in the ability to influence, make a meaningful impact, and serve others. Whether guiding a team, spearheading a project, or simply navigating one's own path, every young person holds the power to lead with grace and conviction. By honing essential leadership qualities, embracing continuous growth, and remaining steadfast in their principles, teenagers can emerge as agents of transformation and sources of inspiration on a global scale.

"Growing Leaders" transcends being merely a book; it serves as a compelling invitation to take decisive steps towards unleashing untapped potential, as well as a profound acknowledgment of the profound impact leadership can have. As individuals who hold positions of influence and guidance, let us pledge to cultivate the upcoming cohort of leaders, equipping them with the tools to enact positive change and establish enduring legacies. Let us unite on this voyage of personal development, education, and leadership, forging a path toward a more promising tomorrow for all.

We express our deepest gratitude for embarking on this remarkable odyssey with us. Let us raise a toast to the future trailblazers, those destined to conquer adversity with unwavering bravery and empathy, and ignite a flame of inspiration that shall guide countless others along their path.

www.ingramcontent.com/pod-product-compliance
Lightning Source LLC
Chambersburg PA
CBHW080850120626

46546CB00008B/2773